Y0-BQN-632

BUSINESS INFORMATION

BUSINESS INFORMATION

How to Find and Use It

By MARIAN C. MANLEY

FORMER BUSINESS LIBRARIAN OF THE PUBLIC LIBRARY OF NEWARK, NEW JERSEY

HARPER & BROTHERS PUBLISHERS NEW YORK

BUSINESS INFORMATION

HOW TO FIND AND USE IT

Printed in the United States of America

FIRST EDITION

K-E

Library of Congress catalog card number: 55-11399

To John Cotton Dana, Beatrice Winser, and John Boynton Kaiser, successive Directors of the Newark Public Library, whose latitude in direction and encouragement of enterprise made possible the work on which this book is based.

contents

Part II. Information Tools for Special Subjects

Part III. The Key to Specific Information

acknowledgments

Because this book is the outcome of thirty years spent in assembling, organizing, and promoting the effective use of data valuable in business development, it is impossible to make due acknowledgment to all who have assisted in its production. Editors, publishers, trade association and government officials, and countless others interested in dissemination of business information have helped in developing knowledge of the field; thousands of users of the Newark Business Library collections have illustrated the manner in which the information may be applied to business problems. The interest in the academic promotion of business information use shown by Rutgers University School of Business Administration, from the dean and faculty to the students, has indicated potential applications of this volume. The constant interchange of inquiry and information among librarians in the field has emphasized its need.

That such a volume is possible is due to the creative imagination of John Cotton Dana who, as director of the Newark Public Library, established its Business Library in 1904. The continuous interest and support given to its development by the city administration and the library trustees has resulted in the work on which this volume is based. Appreciation for immeasurable help must go to members of the staff of the Business Library, whose cooperation through many years has resulted in this and other publications. In the later stages of the work particular assistance was given by Mary P. McLean, Josephine Priestly, and William Stoddard in contributions to the content, and by Louise Byl in secretarial service of high quality. The detailed and constructive criticism of the manuscript by a Chicago business leader, George A. Jones, was of special value. The penetrating comment and enduring patience of Dr. Ordway Tead in the last stages of the work are gratefully acknowledged.

the uses of this book

Skilled use of business data can mean the difference between success or failure in the business world. This book has been compiled to present a picture of the sources of such information and their range. It is based on some thirty years experience as head of the Newark Business Library. Because even now both men of long experience and enterprising beginners are astounded by the information that may be found in print, this book should serve many as the key to invaluable resources. Through it, those fortunate enough to have extensive library collections at their command may be reminded of additional uses. To those remote from publishing centers, the book may be a guide to the accumulation and use of needed data.

Books per se are familiar sources for the study of such business problems as improved methods of personnel management, accounting practices, advertising programs, or market research. But business today has countless other sources of information. Trade association reports and bulletins, government studies, the increasing number of special services that report current trends as they take shape, these along with the trade periodicals and industrial directories are vital tools of business in dealing with the constantly shifting pattern of daily commerce.

In 1904, the first public library department designed to concentrate information most useful to businessmen in one collection in the city's business center was established in Newark, New Jersey. At that time, such publications were few. Neither management nor labor had fully realized the part to be played in economic planning by business print. Now lavish expenditures for a flood of such publications are a recognized expense for large corporations and for many trade unions. But much of this information may be used by the businessman at little outlay if he has some idea of the resources and of the service he may expect from his public library or may secure from many government agencies.

This volume is first of all an introduction to today's varied types of information sources and their application, from the use of films in industry through information as to the channels by which the reader can keep informed on the flow of business books and the sources for their evaluation. Because the use of such information varies widely according to the different occupations, a complete reading by the veteran as well as by the beginner will introduce to or remind the reader of these different sources and indicate the manner in which his competitors may have used them to advantage.

In the chapters devoted to each type of publication, they are discussed at length according to the information they provide, the purposes for which the information may be used, and the channels through which the publications may be found. Since trade and professional men alike, from lawyer to manufacturer or accountant, may at some time need to use these varied media—from directories, services, associations, to the more familiar books and periodicals—each chapter may be of use to all. Emphasis is not placed on particular publications except as illustrations of the range and scope of available information; instead the objective is to open the door to an increasing flow of information, with each new publication finding more receptive readers, because the type to which it belongs has become familiar. Since the book stresses channels for information, it opens the way to the latest compilation of information in all fields.

The volume has three major divisions. Part I discusses the sources and application of business information. It may serve the business novice as an introduction to undreamed-of resources that make for economic progress, and it may remind the veteran of the business world of neglected but valuable tools or call his attention to sources and uses that had heretofore escaped his attention. In the chapters on specific types of publications, it assembles material on present developments and indicates sources of information that will enable the reader to keep in touch with future as well as current data.

Part II consists of chapters listing by subject the major publications mentioned in the introductory section as illustrations of the varied types. Additional sources are included. These references carry detailed information on the contents of the several publications. Since the list is *arranged by subject* it groups all the references on each topic and thus indicates publications on insurance, marketing, finance, and other material.

The third section is a comprehensive index through which all references to a given topic or publication are assembled. Among its features are lists of all mentioned publications of different types, such as directories, periodicals, services, that are grouped by their subject in the list of references and that are mentioned in relation to their use in the introductory section.

Because the chapters on directories, services, trade associations, and government publications all contain references to publications that may be immediately helpful to the banker, lawyer, advertising man, builder, or manufacturer, the bibliography and the index are all-important tools in finding the information touching on a particular business or phase of business activity. Under these specific headings will be found the variety of publications that touch on the hundreds of industries and activities that are part of today's productive efforts.

Through these different sections the book may be used for many purposes. For the reader who wishes a wider knowledge of the varied sources of business information and the manner in which they may be used, it offers comprehensive discussion based on intensive experience. For those seeking specific publications in a particular field, it provides lists of notable current publications besides indicating channels through which further information may be secured. If a selection of outstanding examples of particular publication forms is needed, that too may be found in its pages. Since business is constantly changing and the publications that serve it appear as rapidly as the need emerges, the emphasis is on the manner in which such changes may be followed rather than solely on material already in print.

Since the book is not primarily a selection of the best business tools but instead a description of types of information sources and a guide to the sources of information on all publications, it will lead the reader to forthcoming publications as well as those of current value. Such an approach is essential with the changing demands of business and the rapidly increasing printed tools for its development.

No one collection of material, however large, can contain everything that may be needed at one time or another. But an understanding of the range of business information sources and the part that may be played in economic well-being by libraries, public and private, can be of inestimable value to the individual businessman, novice and veteran alike. This book is the product of thirty years experience in serving business information needs, compiled in the belief that success in meeting these needs is based primarily on a knowledge of the general types of information sources and the manner in which they are used.

part I

THE POWER HOUSE OF BUSINESS PRINT

chapter I

The Why and How of Business Information

Uses of business data. Business and printed information. The public library in the business program. The special librarian as the corporation's information expert.

THE USES OF BUSINESS DATA

The development of information resources and some idea of their extent are obvious to any businessman by reason of the volume of trade magazines that come over his desk, the calls for cooperative effort by his trade association, the government questionnaire that may seem the one job too many for his busy days, or the mail offers of new publications useful in his business. That varied and extensive business data have been accumulated is brought home to him daily. It is the application of this information to his own problem that eludes him.

Often the fact that some vital information has been published is unknown to those who need it most, with the result that time and money are wasted in unnecessary effort. There is the classic story of the president of a large industrial company proudly proclaiming to a friend that $10,000 in travel and consultation fees had been spent to get an essential fact on which to base a plan. The friend looked meditative, and the president next day received a government pamphlet that contained the information it had cost him $10,000 to acquire. That this information was already in print had never occurred to him. Whether or not that story is true, similar situations have arisen and still do. They will occur until the basic principle of checking on published business information before completing plans is established. As technical research has proved, the "literature search" may be half the battle.

BUSINESS AND PRINTED INFORMATION

The many publications for special business use that pour from the presses annually prove that the American businessman has learned the value of recorded experience. The discussions in books and magazines of changing management methods, the statistical compilations available through services and government studies, the guides to markets found in directories, all form part of the reservoir of factual data that he has learned to apply. From the small grocer who, in reading a government survey of grocery operation, discovers the liability involved in carrying too many brands of merchandise, to the public utility statistician who projects developments on the basis of statistical trends, or the specialist in market research who seeks a selected mailing list for a test of consumer reaction, the complex world of business has learned the value of data that can be found in print.

In less than half a century America has seen the development of this reservoir of information. Annual statistics of production and distribution, records of imports and exports by country and kind, commodity prices over the years, index numbers reflecting changes in the cost of living; data such as these have come to be recognized as the basis of business forecasting. Through these compiled facts business has at its command material on which to base long-range plans or to meet today's questions.

No less important than statistical information is knowledge of current trends in business economics, of business methods, and of administrative practice. Changing labor-management relations, the pros and cons of decentralization of industry, marketing's growing pains, consumer analysis, all these and many more have been reported and discussed in business publications. Weighing the value of such discussion has proved essential in saving time and effort.

THE PUBLIC LIBRARY IN THE BUSINESS PROGRAM

As realization of the need for basing business action on factual information has spread, so have channels for information deepened and extended. Through their network the man on the street corner as well as the head of an industry may command unlimited information sources. The keys to this information are in print at any well-equipped public library or may be secured through his own or the library's contacts with other agencies. The limits of his search are only the limits of his enterprise, supplemented by what skill he has acquired in the arts of finding and using information.

Not every businessman has grasped the extent to which library service may be used nor the cooperative relations that exist between libraries themselves and also between libraries and government departments, research organizations, publishers, educational institutions, and other agencies. The public library is the center of a web of information sources and so serves as the community's information contact point. If this aspect has not been fully developed, the lack may be attributed to failure to understand the possibilities of library service on the part of librarians and library users alike. As each group is stimulated by stronger cooperative effort, so will the available information resources come into use for economic progress and the country's welfare.

Where funds rather than time must be saved, the extent and accessibility of public library resources must be weighed. Here the basic principle for all library service must be remembered. It is that the entrance of any library is the approach to a continuing chain of library resources. Through interlibrary loans, through the service of state library agencies, through the cooperation of larger libraries and the Library of Congress, the smallest institution may draw on many more publications than it can house. Before setting this machinery in motion for this wider use, however, the library user should have a clear conception of his own need.

While in Newark, Cleveland, Boston, Chicago, Indianapolis, and some other cities, business library service is developed to a greater extent than in many other institutions, most libraries have much of the same material and are ready to respond to any demand. The businessman's approach to the use of library material may be adversely affected by the time it takes him to understand the library's arrangement of its collection. The progressive library is solving this problem. Where business is interested and strong in the support of a dynamic library service, it may expect that service to conform to its demands, accessibility, selectiveness, and adaptation to rapid use. But business in order to obtain this type of service must make its needs, interests, and convictions on library values clear.

Where libraries have been organized to meet business needs quickly, the user will often find the materials he wants without requiring intervention of library machinery. In many libraries, for example, the user may himself take from the magazine, book, or directory shelves the publication he wants. Assistants familiar with the resources are ready to aid him. But it is not necessary for him to depend on such an intermediary, should he prefer to work directly and without consultation.

The first step is a check on the library's resources to determine whether the necessary business material is available or can be secured. Some businessmen will be sufficiently experienced in the use of a library to know that examination of the catalog may serve their needs. They know too that consultation with the library staff is advisable. Librarians are not only familiar with the special arrangement of their own institutions, but will know what further steps to take. Such steps may involve calling on the resources of other agencies, or by telephone or letter securing supplementary information. On occasion, by furnishing a card of introduction, one library may expedite the inquirer's use of another.

The extent to which library service may be secured by telephone is not always realized. Often the answer to a factual question may be obtained without further effort. Preliminary discussion by telephone will permit the librarian to assemble a selection of appropriate references ready for the inquirer's use when he arrives.

Often the steps taken to meet one inquiry will aid in answering many others, so most progressive librarians advocate an intensive reference service as one means of strengthening their own resources and making the whole information agency a web of greater mutual benefit. Information for one agency may be supplied at some inconvenience, but that very effort may open the door to further much-needed service. The necessary ingredient in any research effort is cooperation, and the library may be counted upon to become an effective link in such cooperation.

The first step for examining the available business books in most libraries will be through the library card catalog. In some places this can be preceded by a study of annotated booklists on special topics. The business divisions of the Newark and Cleveland public libraries issue bulletins covering business publications, focused usually on some current topic. The Newark monthly publication, *Business Literature,* has been issued regularly since 1928, and the Cleveland Public Library's *Business Information Sources* at varying intervals since 1929. Many libraries are subscribers to both publications, and through their columns and the use of other periodicals, a fairly comprehensive evaluation of current business books may be obtained.

With the publication in 1949 of Edwin Coman's *Sources of Business Information,* the general reader, the businessman, the librarian, the research worker acquired a comprehensive guide. Out of the author's wealth of experience as director of Stanford University's Graduate School of Business Library and as instructor in the field of business information sources, he compiled a study that provides a foundation for the use of such data. Although many of the 400 pages are devoted to references on such special topics as real estate, foreign trade, management, finance, there are chapters on the general uses of business information and its application.

While library use is, in varying degrees, a supplement to all school work, skill in drawing on its full resources develops through meeting immediate personal needs. In *Making Books Work,* by Jennie M. Flexner, there is a key that should not be overlooked. A compact, readable little volume, it discusses library procedures from the point of view of the library user and clarifies for him the purpose of such mystifying processes as library cataloging. Too, general reference books and their special service in meeting different questions are discussed in such graphic detail as to open new avenues of information not only to the inexperienced library visitor but to the habitué.

Another current publication that clarifies the procedures in assembling information so as to insure adequate records of sources is *The Research Paper* by Hook and Gaver. In this the basic steps in using library resources are outlined, together with the techniques for organizing material in a coherent pattern.

THE SPECIAL LIBRARIAN AS THE CORPORATION'S INFORMATION EXPERT

It is debatable at what stage of development a business organization should employ an information expert. As time goes on it is recognized that any organization ready to profit by the use of recorded experience needs to centralize responsibility for information. Some one person must both know the information sources already developed in the organization and serve as the contact through which the library and other information resources are reached. Information accessible through periodicals, through trade association contacts, through specialized services, in pamphlets, by special mailings, and through the daily newspapers is a part of every business. Selection and assimilation of what is useful to the concern must follow if the expenditures are to bear fruit. Too, efficient use must be made of the information resources without its doors; the public, college, and special libraries.

In many progressive organizations, this information expert will be the librarian. A background of public library experience and professional education may bring the best results. The skills required to organize information resources effectively can be acquired most rapidly from such a background. Qualified people may be secured by consulting the local librarian, the placement offices of the various library schools, or the placement divisions of the American Library Association or the Special Libraries Association.

The proved procedure in setting up an information contact point or library for an organization is to find the right person, put all information sources under her jurisdiction, give her adequate funds and authority to develop the best setup for the particular organization, and expect results. In no two situations will the conditions be the same, and so flexibility in outlook and development are necessary.

The "special library" is an important development in many efficiently operated organizations. Its numbers have increased in proportion to the growing awareness of the value found in the expert use of recorded information. These special libraries vary from a few files of pamphlets and magazines in the care of a smart young woman with a wide knowledge of information contacts on which she may call, to the elaborate research library, spaciously housed and with a large staff. An illuminating picture of the extent to which such intensive collections of published material have been developed is found in the bulky three volumes of *Special Library Resources,* a monumental effort of the Special Libraries Association. Another record of the functions and materials involved in special library service in different occupations from newspaper offices to financial institutions, chemical plants, or commercial firms is given in *The Special Library Profession and What It Offers,* published by that association.

chapter II

Business Information and Its Application

Information sources for special needs. Suggestions for investigating an industry's possibilities. Aids in selecting a home community. Finding data on individuals.

INFORMATION SOURCES FOR SPECIAL NEEDS

Business information sources fall into several broad classes; the relative usefulness of each depends upon the occupation of the user. The general sources of business information are directories, magazines, services, trade association publications, government publications, books, yearbooks, encyclopedias, and the pamphlets or books published by organizations working in special fields. Business magazines carry the story of changing methods in meeting continuing problems, list the market records that indicate the costs of production, report on new developments, and in general reflect the ever-changing pattern of industry today. Services are developed to meet particular needs in special fields and are adapted to their purpose through publication format and timing. Trade directories open the door to markets and to sources of study, and reflect the status of a particular industry and those it serves. Government reports, in their utilization of nationwide questionnaires, return to the businessman in usable form the over-all average by which his progress may be measured. Trade associations, by cooperative effort, provide data on the problems best solved through united action. Book publishers note recurring questions and provide the answer in texts that, through their intensive treatment of different phases of business activity, aid in progress. All the publications and their contents form part of the great reservoir of information at the disposal of the executive aware of the power that lies in effective use of print.

SUGGESTIONS FOR INVESTIGATING AN INDUSTRY'S POSSIBILITIES

When time for systematic study is available, an investigation of an industry might follow these steps. First, consulting a general encyclopedia and, if possible, the *Encyclopedia of the Social Sciences.* This will give a general background and a guide to supplementary reading. Examination of current reports of the industry in the investment services such as Standard & Poor's or Moody's or Fitch might follow for the record of its size and distribution, its condition over a period of years, and its ramifications. With this foundation of background information, a further step is examination of the periodicals published in the interests of the industry. Too, the trade directories in the field are useful as a guide to the size and distribution of the industry's units.

For years the federal government has cooperated with business in assembling and compiling information. Both through questionnaires to industrial concerns and through cooperation with trade associations, a wealth of statistical and informative material has been assembled, compiled, interpreted, and transmitted to the business users by the government departments and the government printing press. Careful study of such publications insures basic understanding of established conditions and possible trends in the industry. Trade associations also assemble and compile information on the industry's progress. Contact with all these sources will result in much enlightening data.

Invaluable to the man going into business for himself are the pamphlets in the *Establishing and Operating Series,* which may be obtained from the Superintendent of Documents in Washington or from any field office of the Department of Commerce. These satisfying little books do not pretend to offer technical instruction, but offer advice on the business operation of an enterprise, both before launching it and also after it has become well established. When considering the establishment of a business, the prospective proprietor, if he is alert, should inquire whether a book of this kind, covering his chosen field, has been published by the Department of

Commerce. To those already in business, these publications may propose solutions to some of their dilemmas. The practical suggestions which they contain are definitely slanted toward the small businesman.

AIDS IN SELECTING A HOME COMMUNITY

Another frequent question that touches many lives is the selection of a home site. Such selection may be forced by the acceptance of a new position, with the related necessity for moving a comfortably established family from one city to another. To find the right community surroundings for the new home means judging relative advantages and disadvantages. Available information in such a dilemma is just as complete and varied as in the case of industry research.

Again, the search may start with the encyclopedia. The *Americana,* for example, gives United States cities fairly extensive treatment, and such reading will provide an over-all picture. The past few years have seen the development of many studies in market analysis as applied to communities. Condensed statements on the communities served by daily papers appear in *Editor and Publisher Market Guide*. Other statistical data on standards of living are found in *Sales Management* annual *Survey of Buying Power,* covering a large number of localities and containing a guide to the relative cost of living through composite index numbers. Basic statistics for such market analysis are compiled from the census publication and through special analysis by the publishers of the magazine. A helpful descriptive listing of many sources of community information, "Where to Work and Live," appeared in the Newark Library's *Business Literature,* Vol. XVIII, No. 1.

The investment manuals disclose the financial standing of various municipalities through inclusion in reports on securities of data on tax rates, growth of funded debt, changes in assessed valuations, etc. Chambers of Commerce specialize in providing community information, and their enthusiastic claims may be checked and analyzed through use of the factual information available elsewhere.

City directories are important sources of information. Their value as records of community change and the uses for their information are discussed at length in "City Directories as Economic and Sociological Records" in *Business Literature,* Vol. XXIII, No. 7. Almost any city directory includes a statement of the local growth and general trends. Comparison of such data over a period of years focuses attention on the economic and growth factors in a city's development.

The basic source of community information is the census. These volumes record the composition of the population in age, national origins, educational, and occupational division. The statistics are often broken down into small sections. Too, business and professional directories contain helpful information. The school and the library directories indicate cultural resources. The geographic index of *Who's Who in America* lists the leaders of the community, while the geographic index of *Poor's Register of Directors and Executives* reflects the economic level. In addition, the industries of an area are designated in the geographical section of *McKittrick's Directory of Advertisers.* Here too the federal government has made many contributions to the available information on particular communities. A broad conception of the social and economic characteristics of any area may be secured through these publications, while the extensive information available in the volumes on states and cities published under the sponsorship of the Federal Writers' Project stimulate interest in these data.

FINDING DATA ON INDIVIDUALS

A third major question often asked, that which seeks information about an individual, is more difficult to answer. Information on people is less easily assembled than that on places or industries. Its availability is in direct relation to the prominence of the person involved. The many special biographical dictionaries in different professions, such as engineering, banking, commerce and industry, law, medicine, etc., supplement *Who's Who in America.* The professional directories are valuable but are limited in number. Association journals are a help; membership listings are useful, footnotes in magazines about authors of articles furnish valuable sidelights on people in public affairs. Examples of information appearing in unexpected sources are the biographical notes on public speakers, such as given in "Speakers for Sales Meetings. Where to Get Them" in the "Sales Meetings and Conventions" section of the Dartnell Corporation's *Sales Methods Series.*

Some information on individuals is recorded in city directories. The detail varies with the different directory publishers. Often the listing includes the occupation, the name of the wife, a record of removal, and other notes that simplify identification. Home neighborhoods, business affiliations as indicated through the directory, and other personal items all help to form a miniature biography.

Seldom are all these sources of personal information available in any one place. The public library may serve as a contact point for sources not already available there. Libraries are linked by bonds of mutual assistance, and the staff will either initiate inquiries or advise the inquirer on the next step in the investigation. In Ohio, for example, if the librarian of a small town were approached for special information she would be likely to refer the inquirer to the Business Information Bureau of Cleveland. Here expert service and a magnificent collection would enable the inquirer to secure much desired information. If the search were unsuccessful, the Business Information Bureau staff would in turn communicate with other sources of information, such as government departments, a trade association, or another library. Ohio is fortunate in the possession of this service, as is Massachusetts in Boston's Kirstein Business Library. In the New York metropolitan area, the Newark Business Library is the chief information center of this type. However, all public libraries are ingenious in developing ways to provide information. In the rare cases where a library fails to procure what is needed, the businessman may find help through his trade association or through the Department of Commerce regional offices and other agencies.

chapter III

Meeting the Individual's Business Information Needs

A ready reference library. Useful statistical compilations. Check lists for the desk library. Meeting the secretary's needs.

In meeting his information needs, the businessman has two and sometimes three alternatives. One is the development of the individual's ready reference shelf; another is the use of the public library. The third—less frequently—is the appointment of an information expert or special librarian for the business.

If, as his first step, he decides on a desk library, the executive must evaluate the different publications and decide which should be immediately at hand. Where time or distance enter into the picture, there are general business information compilations that, at his desk, will save valuable hours. The special needs of the individual determine the precise selection of his essential publications.

A READY REFERENCE LIBRARY

First, in this desk library comes a general information handbook such as the *World Almanac,* or the *Information Please Almanac.* These contain information on cities, census figures, governmental organizations, data on foreign countries, and other facts needed on occasion. While such information may be used infrequently, even occasional use may save a surprising amount of valuable time and effort.

In a day of increasing government participation in private enterprise, it is necessary to have ready access to information about the federal government. *The Congressional Directory* gives names and addresses of federal officials and agencies, and the *U.S. Government Organization Manual* explains the complex setup of government and interprets the functions of its divisions.

USEFUL STATISTICAL COMPILATIONS

In the decade and a half since the depression, the increasing tendency to apply methods of analysis to business procedures, the growing power of organized labor, and the widespread effort to determine the basic causes for economic fluctuations have created a strong demand for statistical data. In an era when negotiated wage agreements are front-page news, changes in the consumer price index, for example, create widespread interest.

A publication that provides a store of data is the *Statistical Abstract*. Since for all tables it lists the original sources, this treasured volume with its statistical records of all kinds is not only an invaluable compilation of information but a guide to additional material. In its exposition of the many agencies whose cooperation makes possible an informed business world, it is revealing and highly satisfactory.

Another statistical handbook for desk use is the annual *Economic Almanac* published by the National Industrial Conference Board. This volume, a by-product of that organization's many years of fact finding and fact furnishing, contains economic and industrial statistical data not only for recent periods but also over a long span of years. Because of the organization's extensive work in cost-of-living studies, individual savings, and national wealth, data on those subjects are particularly comprehensive and enlightening. All in all, it has proved an outstanding success in meeting its objective to provide a compact, convenient handbook of the latest, most significant, and trustworthy statistical data.

Important basic tools in business research containing authoritative economic data pertaining to the over-all picture of business are the supplements to the *Survey of Current Business* published monthly by the U.S. Department of Commerce. These supplements provide a comprehensive statistical record of business activity since 1935. *Business Statistics* is published every two years, and the data selected for this supplement are those which have most bearings on the current operation of the business community. Here may be found that most quoted of statistics, the consumer price index. Changes in this figure as well as other basic statistics are recorded in the weekly statistical supplements to *Survey of Current Business.* Another supplement to *Survey of Current Business* is the *National Income* edition, usually published in February, which summarizes business activity for the preceding year.

The value of these slim blue paper-bound books, which can be obtained at nominal cost from any Department of Commerce field office or the Superintendent of Documents in Washington, cannot be overestimated. Not only are these federal government compilations accurate, up-to-date, and authoritative, but their presentation of material on a comparative basis makes them valuable indicators of business trends and industrial changes. However much the layman may shun statistical sheets, the businessman should know this annual review number of the *Survey of Current Business* where, sandwiched between tables and graphs, he will almost certainly find a readable summary of business conditions having direct bearing on his own business activity.

As an over-all picture of all industry, and a guide to various current publications serving the different fields, few volumes surpass the annual *Market Data* issue of *Industrial Marketing.* For each major industry, it summarizes statistical data, current trends and developments, and many special details. Along with such information it lists the names and addresses of the related trade associations. Each industry's special publications, both periodicals and directories, are recorded, together with their circulation, format, and advertising rates. All in all, this volume not only gives for the United States and Canada the current record of each industry in summarized form, but lists the publications that service it, and points the way to additional sources of information.

In this field of statistics, a magazine supplement having special value is the annual *Survey of Buying Power* published by *Sales Management,* the magazine of marketing. This estimates the buying income of metropolitan and rural areas and gives a detailed analysis of the nationwide retail sales of principal products during the preceding year. Another such study, the annual *Consumer Markets* of *Standard Rate and Data Service,* has detailed marketing data on all cities over 5000 population.

Another magazine, *Editor and Publisher,* in its two annual issues, the *Market Guide* and the *International Yearbook,* has compiled a wide range of information to meet particular needs. The first of these provides a survey of 1450 daily newspaper markets, indicating for each the type of community, the principal industries, the estimated payrolls, the educational institutions, the newspapers, and other essential facts. The second is an exhaustive guide to newspapers, their personnel, and affiliated groups, and furnishes leads to sources influential in developing public opinion.

CHECK LISTS FOR THE DESK LIBRARY

A guide to current publications in business fields and one that reflects current information demands, *Business Literature,* published ten times a year by the Business Library of the Newark Public Library, has many uses. The ten-year compilation, *Business Literature, 1934-1944,* and the supplementary issues, list and describe periodicals, services, directories, books, and pamphlets; record government and association activities that concern themselves with current business trends; and so indicate what questions are currently under consideration in the business world.

Since 1930 the Industrial Relations Section of Princeton University has issued, in successive editions, a bibliographical pamphlet entitled *The Office Library of an Industrial Relations Executive.* The selection of titles is based upon such subjects as Personnel Administration, Labor Legislation and Administration, and Social Insurance. The last chapter contains a list of reference handbooks.

However constant or infrequent their use, these publications not only provide, in small compass and at modest cost, an incalculable amount of important current information, but also show the way to supplementary material. A similar list of useful aids, "Desk Library of Information Sources for the Businessman," appeared in Vol. XIX, No. 7 of *Business Literature,* published by the Newark Public Library.

MEETING THE SECRETARY'S NEEDS

An efficient secretary needs certain books within easy reach, and of prime importance is a secretary's handbook. Many of these are listed in *Business Literature,* Vol. XXI, No. 6, which features "The Secretary's Reference Kit." A useful but little known addition to the desk library is Howard Measure's *Styles of Address,* stating correct usages in addressing such diverse figures as congressmen, college deans, and peers.

Gold mines of ready information on names and locations so often desired quickly by businessmen are the *U.S. Official Postal Guide* and *Standard Advertising Register.* The former, far more than a statement of postal regulations, is an excellent source of geographical information, and the latter, although intended primarily for the advertiser, has information on 13,000 companies, giving their location and the names of officers. Its company list, classified by product, makes it useful as a purchasing guide and an index of trademarks. The *Standard Advertising Register,* published by the National Register Publishing Company of New York City, has as additional features, geographical and alphabetical lists of advertising agencies with their officers and clients. The *Standard Advertising Register* is one of the most used volumes in the business section of the public library, and supplements would more than repay their costs in many offices.

chapter IV

Business Magazines—The Record of Changing Trends

Meeting the industry's demands. Magazines for special needs. Evaluation of editorial content. Relation of an industry to its periodicals. Advertising as a measure of vitality. Guides to magazine selection. Aids in use of periodicals. House organs—periodicals for the individual enterprise.

Around 1935-37 a committee composed of editors, trade association executives, government officials, and librarians carried on a study of the relative use of different business information sources. In its course, the presidents of a thousand leading business organizations in different fields were asked what steps they took in securing needed data. Of the 500 replies to the questionnaires, the large majority listed the business and trade press as the first source to which they turned for information on any business problem. In view of the wide diversification and comprehensive coverage in the business paper field, such findings do not come as a surprise. Magazines for every industry and for every division of industry, for interests common to all, such as purchasing, advertising, sales, labor policies, come from the press in a steady stream. Out of this mass of published material, to find the most useful periodical for a special need calls for more than casual investigation.

MEETING THE INDUSTRY'S DEMANDS

The broad interpretation of an industry in its periodicals indicates both the trend of developments and the ever-changing methods and scope of operations. The more specific details of corporate activity and current conditions, production, distribution, management, and labor relations are all reflected in the columns of the trade press. Their statistical records, over a period of years, show the industry's rate of expansion. The tone of the comment on labor relations, government contacts, research methods, reflects generally accepted policies.

These periodicals are almost invariably the best sources of information on latest developments in the ever-changing structure of economics and industry. Current aspects of such important activities as legislation, taxation, union negotiations, convention news, and personnel practices are described most fully in business magazines. They contain biographies of outstanding businessmen and are the media for exchange of marketing information and merchandising ideas. Often they are the only sources for histories of individual companies, product development, and improvement. Magazines issued by the government first publish the statistics, which later are the basis for authoritative reports and full-length books.

The form and content of any magazine result from its function as a current reporting medium. To meet specific needs, statistical data such as business failures, department store sales, car loadings, electric power output, cost of living changes, income tax returns, and many other business indicators are necessary. Market prices of products must be referred to constantly. Notes on production, distribution, changing demand are all important. Listings briefly noting personnel have proved valuable. Specific and accurate material on methods is essential. Where government regulation is in effect, the editorial content should reflect accurate, impartial attitudes on such matters as affect the development of the industry. In striving to "eliminate in so far as possible his personal opinions from his news columns, but to be a leader of thought in his editorial columns and to make his criticisms constructive," the business paper editor must steer a wisely chosen course.

In recent years these magazines have broadened their appeal through spectacular use of photography and the new processes in color lithography. Some apply the eye-arresting techniques of good advertising layout. In both content and format, they employ many of the same devices as the consumer publications, and the readers of *Women's Wear Daily* read news of the latest New York shows as well as the trade names of the new textiles.

Few people realize the tremendous coverage of the so-called trade publications, and visitors to the Newark Business Library are frequently amazed when they discover such titles as *Tea and Coffee Trade Journal, India Rubber World, Soybean Digest, Coin Machine Review, Candy Merchandising, American Dry Cleaner, Wallpaper Journal, American Cemetery, Packaging Parade, Wines and Spirits, Macaroni Journal,* and *Jersey Rabbit Journal.* It is almost no exaggeration to state that "whatever the business, there is a magazine published about it." Such periodicals are not only guides to wholesale and retail purchasing and marketing products, but also contain news of the trade, which often furnishes the best over-all picture of current activities.

MAGAZINES FOR SPECIAL NEEDS

Some business publications serve to keep the reader in touch with over-all industrial development. Conspicuous in this field is the national magazine *Business Week.* Both for its succinct and illuminating reporting of current business developments and for its longer special studies, it is an invaluable guide to the changing business scene. Its "Business Barometer" with its supporting statistical data is a graphic portrayal of week-to-week conditions. Another periodical that takes high place as enlivening and provocative reading is *Changing Times,* the Kiplinger publication. This magazine with wide general appeal can be as highly recommended to the small retailer as to the president of a large corporation. *Fortune,* that plutocrat of the business press, is a dramatic, monumental presentation of business Titans, equally as stirring in its treatment of the wheatfields of the plains as of the mysteries of science applied to industry's advancement.

Many trade journals issue annual survey and directory numbers which may serve as excellent reference books for the trade. Other trade journals devote special numbers to one phase of activity. Fields as extensive as accounting, banking, and insurance with their ramifications are covered by numerous periodicals. With national interest focused on the employer-employee relationship, there has been an increase in the number of magazines devoted to personnel and management problems. Examples of these are *Personnel, Personnel Journal,* and *Advanced Management.*

Magazines containing information essential to an understanding of business reflect the varied groups who publish them, both in content and format. Among authoritative business publications sponsored by universities are the *Harvard Business Review,* published bimonthly by the Graduate School of Business Administration, Harvard University, and the quarterly *Journal of Business of the University of Chicago.*

The federal government itself publishes several magazines combining basic data with latest reports on foreign trade and on business and industrial development. These include *Survey of Current Business* and its supplements, *Foreign Commerce Weekly* published by the U.S. Department of Commerce, and the *Federal Reserve Bulletin* issued monthly by the Board of Governors of the Federal Reserve System. Also important are the *Statistical Bulletin* of the Securities and Exchange Commission, the United Nations *Monthly Bulletin of Statistics,* and the *Monthly Labor Review* published by the U.S. Department of Labor. The importance of these government issued periodicals cannot be overestimated, since their content is official, accurate, and up to the minute, and their editors have become increasingly aware of the necessity of making them both attractive and easily understood by the layman.

EVALUATION OF EDITORIAL CONTENT

The contents of specific business papers result from and are responsive to the needs of the particular industries. The finished product reflects the editorial and fact-gathering methods that provide the current information essential to its various activities. Because of the reportorial standards that must be set up to meet demands so exacting, some understanding of what is offered by the best is advisable. That understanding may easily be secured by a study of the publications themselves. This will develop a personal familiarity with their contents, the adequacy of their editorial comments, and the many features that are valuable aids to the industrial reader. McGraw-Hill Publishing Company is perhaps the leader in the business paper field, with some twenty-seven periodicals ranging from *American Machinist* through *Power.* Other publishers also show diversification in their coverage. This is illustrated by Simmons-Boardman with *American Builder* and *Railway Age;* Chilton Publications with *Distribution Age* and *Hardware Age,* and Conover-Mast publications with *Purchasing* and *Mill and Factory.*

In considering the relative value of various periodicals, certain points may be checked. Is the reputation of the publishing company good? What is the editorial experience of those directing the policies of the periodical? How current is the information? Is there an undue lag between the assembled information and its publication? How comprehensive is its coverage? If statistics are given, what periods do they embrace? Is the geographic range broad or limited, general or detailed? An important question in weighing the usefulness of a publication is: Is it biased? Do the editor's or owner's policies and practices color his publication? Where do its sources of support lie? Has the magazine a record for editorial integrity?

Constructive effort to aid in the promotion and welfare of industry is a vital principle of the trade press. Both the Associated Business Papers and the National Conference of Business Paper Editors have stimulated constructive editorial and publishing policies. Members of the Associated Business Papers subscribe to such ethical standards of publishing practice as these:

1. To consider first the interest of the subscriber.
2. To eliminate, in so far as possible, his personal opinions from his news columns, but to be a leader of thought in his editorial columns and to make his criticism constructive.
3. To refuse to publish "puffs," free reading notices, or paid writeups; to keep his reading columns independent of advertising consideration, and to measure all news by this standard: "Is it real news?"

That these standards have proved effective is shown by the marked improvement in the business press over the years.

A major contribution in clarifying problems and objectives was the publication by the Associated Business Papers of *The Business Paper Editor at Work* by Douglas Woolf. This stimulating volume, as an exposition of the methods and responsibility of the editor, is valuable reading for the business reader since it throws light on the wide range of contact and activities involved.

RELATION OF AN INDUSTRY TO ITS PERIODICALS

A good yardstick of the condition of an industry lies in its periodical literature. Magazines of high editorial content, substantial quality, and good circulation indicate vitality and expansion. The banking business, for example, has supported its trade press for more than sixty years. It has ably edited not only several periodicals of good standing and national circulation, but others specializing in regional service. Some industries of recent but vigorous development have produced magazines with notable editorial programs. The history and trends in these fields are shown in *Business Journalism, its Function and Future* by Julian Elfenbein.

While competition has been influential in raising the standards of the business press as corporate or individual enterprises, some valuable publications are underwritten and published by associations. Illustrations are *Nation's Business,* the mouthpiece of the United States Chamber of Commerce, and *Banking,* issued by the American Bankers' Association.

ADVERTISING AS A MEASURE OF VITALITY

The advertising pages, as the lifeblood of the business press, reveal the progress of industry. While they are the measure of success of the business publisher, that success can be sustained only by editorial content of high quality. If this fails, the magazine is certain to meet decreasing interest on the part of the reader who seeks wide coverage for his industry, and circulation, as a result, suffers. The advertising manager, the circulation manager, and the editor all seek to produce a publication that will retain both advertiser and reader interest, since each is essential for the journal's progress. Quality can be maintained only by taking advantage of close observation of the industry's needs.

Today the quality of the American business press has advanced to a degree that can be a matter of national satisfaction. There is in that press some particular development that is most vitally related to the day-by-day activities of the alert business executive. It is not only his obligation but an educational opportunity to take advantage of such a business asset!

GUIDES TO MAGAZINE SELECTION

The businessman who wants to be in touch with current reading matter most suited to his needs must consider both the time at his disposal and the effective use of funds. In one way or another many business papers are brought to his attention. Of those which should he see regularly, which should he read intermittently and what reading may he delegate to others? As a help in deciding what magazines he wants at his desk and which he would like to feel are available to him on call, an examination of the public library's selected collection will be of value.

To find the publications that treat of many special phases, another tool is needed, the classified list of business magazines. The businessman who is already familiar with *Industrial Marketing*'s *Market Data Book* will have one such index at his command. Others are worthy of special attention for the varying degrees with which they meet such needs.

The most current and inclusive but least descriptive list is that foundation stone for periodical and newspaper records, *Ayer's*. This directory lists geographically newspapers and magazines by state and county, giving their individual characteristics, date established, frequency, size, and circulation. It includes also a broadly classified list of trade, technical, and class publications which provide current reading from advertising to zoology and including mail order trade, real estate, and other business topics.

The second list particularly useful for its international coverage and convenient for its grouping under broad general subjects is Ulrich's *Periodicals Directory*. This classified list contains some 7500 entries under topics from accounting through biology, and other general subjects. Its particular value for business use is as a guide for foreign as well as domestic publications in commerce and industry. Its close index to subjects as well as to specific publications adds to its value. Each entry gives the title, subtitle, date of origin, frequency, price, publisher, place of publication, and information on whether the publication has illustrations, supplements, special numbers, or a yearbook. Some publications issued by government departments and state universities, as well as some house organs, are included.

The *Editorial Directory*, first published in 1952, is especially designed to provide information on the editorial content and the personnel of the magazines it lists. The directory is divided into three main sections: business, industrial, and professional publications; farm publications; and consumer publications. Each of these sections is again subdivided into groups by interests. With its detailed information on each periodical and its division by interest, it is especially valuable as a tool for magazine selection.

These lists are guides to current business publications. What each of the magazines contains that meets a businessman's particular needs calls for his special consideration. A general practice is to select for regular reading a magazine that gives over-all treatment of current business conditions, another filling the same function for his industry, and a publication that specializes in his particular department or section of the industry. Too, he must decide on the publications in related fields with which he should be conversant. Among the periodicals essential for all business, advertising magazines are of special value as secondary reading for general information. Many new developments, new publications, new methods are touched on in their columns; close attention to the reports in the trade press is necessary to maintain familiarity with current business policies that are going to affect procedures for coming months, years, or perhaps permanently.

AIDS IN USE OF PERIODICALS

With several good magazines at hand, what tools for their use will be found most helpful? Probably the most important single key to the continuing stream of print is *Public Affairs Information Service*, or *PAIS*, with its bulletins and periodic cumulations. This provides a weekly index to the new books, current periodicals, government documents, and pamphlets in the field of economics and public affairs published in all English-speaking countries. In an enlivening brochure *How to Save $4900*, the basis of selection of 500 appropriate entries for one week from some 3000 to 6000 articles, pamphlets, and books, is described. While not a necessary tool for every business man, some idea of the scope of *PAIS* should be ascertained, and an occasional examination of an issue will prove of value.

Two other indexes, found in more libraries than *PAIS*, are *Industrial Arts Index* and *Readers Guide to Periodical Literature.* These two familiar guides are comprehensive in their coverage of the magazines that they index. Their cumulation into volumes covering five-year intervals makes a review of the references to a subject a comparatively rapid task.

An important supplement to these various publications is the *New York Times Index,* with its particular value in dating business developments. So much business news is now reported in the daily press that this *Index* will prove not only an approach to the columns of the *Times* but also a guide to the period in which magazine discussion of the topic may be anticipated. In that the *Index* is an important tool.

HOUSE ORGANS—PERIODICALS FOR THE INDIVIDUAL ENTERPRISE

A type of business magazine often overlooked as a source of business information is the house organ or company-sponsored publication. According to *Printers' Ink Directory of House Organs,* the best listing of such publications, there were approximately 5552 different house organs published in 1950. House organs are of two kinds: some are intended primarily for company employees only, while others circulate outside the company to customers, trade associates, and other interested parties.

With morale building as a prime objective, some merely chronicle employee social and sports events. Columns of personal notes emphasize close relationship between management and employee. House organs intended for employees on the distribution end of business, such as sales staff, distributors, dealers, and customers usually are concerned with selling goods and services. Many of these publications explain new display ideas, give consumer testimonials, print selling talks, and offer specific data on new markets. Improved production is usually the purpose of company magazines addressed to workers in manufacturing and processing, and these may provide details on new production methods and machines, report labor-management agreements, and may relate the company's role in the war effort.

The house organ with a circulation outside the company has promotional and educational aims. By describing the activities of a company as they affect the general public, they may create good will. A file of house organs will reflect what many companies have done to eliminate absenteeism, to commend loyalty, to encourage sports, hobbies, and social activities, and to set up welfare and benefit programs. They contain information on pension plans, safety devices, and employee participation in civic affairs. More than any publication, they reflect the current effort of employer to meet employee on a common ground. These publications may meet the need of the executive who complains that "he is tired of theory and wants to know what really works."

chapter V

Directories as Sources of Business Information

The range of directory information. Finding the right directory. Trade directories as a reflection of industrial change. Publication problems in meeting information needs. Directories with many functions. Directories as aids in identifying trademarks. Varied uses of the city directory.

THE RANGE OF DIRECTORY INFORMATION

Who is the trust officer of the First National Bank in Phoenix, Arizona? What daily paper in Charlotte, North Carolina, has the largest circulation? Does Martin's in Sioux City have a New York buyer? What advertising agency has the Yale & Towne account? Which is the largest hotel in Williamsport?

These and half a hundred other questions are answered through an expanding information source, trade directories. These publications, along with industrial catalogs, professional directories, membership lists, services, all are useful in providing such information as names of officials, professional men, manufacturers, their addresses, products by kind, and other market information. Such widely differing compilations as the *Standard Advertising Register* with its selective lists of leading advertisers in many industries, and of the major advertising agencies and their accounts; and *Martindale-Hubbell* with its record of lawyers by state, represent two versions of these information sources.

Trade directories provide a comprehensive guide to varied commercial activities and their diversified personnel. The majority cover only a specific industry. Others include lists that touch on many different fields. Trade directories such as *Thomas' Register of American Manufacturers, Ayer's Directory of Newspapers and Periodicals,* or *Standard Advertising Register* are typical of such widely useful publications. Because they are comprehensive and detailed, they give nationwide answers to such questions as who makes what, what is published where, and what companies are leaders in many fields.

FINDING THE RIGHT DIRECTORY

Many directories are so specialized as to be used only occasionally. A large collection, covering all professions and industries, should be available for consultation in any market area. The public library of the region's market center is the logical place in which such a collection should be found. If the library has experienced little demand for such information, some consultation with the librarian may be advisable in urging the establishment of a useful collection of this type. Library officials are glad to develop their materials to meet specific information needs, and cooperative discussion may be relied upon to produce satisfactory results.

Extensive collections of trade directories are not found in all public libraries. Some libraries have failed to realize their value as an essential part of business information service, and so have not employed them in the most effective way as a unit. Comprehensive collections, it is true, are found in the large city libraries emphasizing service to business. These libraries stress the trade directory as an important business tool. While as yet such collections are not the rule, almost any city or town library stands ready to assemble a trade directory collection when encouraged to do so by its business community. But encouragement is needed. Local cooperation may spark the beginning of such a collection or supplement the library purchases by gifts.

American Business Directories issued by the Department of Commerce, gives a general listing of current directories. More restricted current information is published yearly in *Industrial Marketing's Market Data Book.* Another current guide to annual publications is in *Public Affairs Information Service,* which lists each year in its annual volume under the heading "trade directories" all entries that have appeared in the weekly issues. A selective annotated list of the trade directories in more frequent use appears in the Appendix of *Business and the Public Library*. Through one channel or another much attention has been focused on these invaluable aids to business information and the many efforts made to bring into general use the resources they offer.

Trade directories are used to find specific facts, whether it is to trace the source of a product or the development of a mass market. Information may be needed about the location of the nearest manufacturer of some commodity or machine. Such a need may be met by using the classified listings in *Thomas' Register*. Again the development of a market for certain products may be under consideration. Trade directories for industries using the product will provide the answer. These volumes often give such close breakdowns for industries as to permit concentration of effort on the divisions that form the possible market. Too, regional analysis for testing a market is possible through a combination of these directories.

Business needs are varied, and the publications evolved to meet them are many. In the use of trade directories, as in other information sources, a basic principle is to assume that such directory information may be found in print. To verify this a consultation with the organization's information expert, the special librarian, with the librarian of the local public library, or with any one of the heads of the specialized business information departments in such public libraries as Boston, Chicago, Cleveland, and Newark may be helpful. Where information of this type has been in constant use over a long period, expert advice is available on the combination of publications that will meet the need.

TRADE DIRECTORIES AS A REFLECTION OF INDUSTRIAL CHANGE

Trade directory pages must be studied for more than surface information. The record of any industry will reflect the changes in its growth. Not only will actual increase in the number of manufacturers of a given product be shown in successive editions of the directory, but also any shift in geographic distribution. The increase in classification and in the variety of products, the development in terminology, the changing trends in mechanization—these and many other shifts in the history of an industry may be discovered through close analysis of its directory publications.

PUBLICATION PROBLEMS IN MEETING INFORMATION NEEDS

Since the demand is limited, and the processes of compilation and publication are costly, directories are often expensive. The information presented in each varies with the industry and the demand, but comprehensive detail is a frequent feature. Directories are not lightly produced, and some of them, because of the extent of the information they have included, have been too expensive to warrant their continuance.

Trade directories have developed out of the pressing need for information on the personnel and distribution of various industries. Many are the logical outcome of the subscription lists and diversified information gathered through the development of trade magazines. The McGraw-Hill electrical trade journals with their by-product, the *Electrical Buyers Reference,* an industry catalog and directory, illustrates publications that reflect that outgrowth. Directories are a normal and useful end product of the knowledge of companies, their personnel, and markets. Through the existing channels open to him, therefore, the periodical publisher is in the best position to secure information and sift it out for inclusion in the trade directory.

The Fairchild Company and the Lockwood Company exemplify organizations that have efficiently combined magazine and directory publishing. Their techniques differ materially, however. Lockwood produces a substantial volume covering the widespread paper industry in great detail, and charges accordingly. Fairchild, in serving the retail trade and garment industry, with its rapid turnover, shifts in population, and constant change in personnel, produces small, ephemeral volumes with limited information on specific companies, but covering a great number of classifications.

Trade directories vary from the little paper-covered adjunct to some journal in a restricted field to a substantial publication such as *Polk's Banker's Encyclopedia,* dealing with businesses running into the millions, listing officers, resources, affiliated institutions, and other pertinent information. Another directory that is a by-product of editorial activity in the investment field is *Poor's Register of Directors and Executives.*

A directory that grew out of an advertising agency's activities to become an essential reference book in all libraries and a basic tool in many other fields is *Ayer's Newspaper Directory.* Here periodicals and newspapers are grouped first by states and cities, then listed alphabetically by name. Information for each publication includes publisher, circulation, political leanings, date and frequency, subscription rates, etc. Another advantage is a broadly classified listing of publications by type. Besides this material it includes concise gazetteer information on states, but particularly on cities, including the principal industries and their general characteristics.

Trade directories represent every type of occupation and intertest, and their costs are as varied as their coverage. Frequency of publishing dates depends on the extent of the demand. The range of information included and the resulting cost of the publication reflect the stability of the industry in its various units. Trade directories are not published on the basis of such standards of quality, content, and form as have been established for dictionaries and encyclopedias, although in their use they compare with such publications. They have evolved from the actual business necessity of letting possible customers know where certain materials may be produced and to open the way to sources of needed commodities. Like periodicals, their income is drawn from the sale of space in the publication as well as the sale of the book itself.

DIRECTORIES WITH MANY FUNCTIONS

The *Standard Advertising Register* described as a service is really important primarily for its directory information. It groups leading advertisers by different industries, listing for each company the officers, the advertising managers, the advertising appropriation, and the type of media used. This particular volume can serve as a selective list of the major companies in all industries. It reveals the most progressive companies, their location and products, as well as information about their personnel. Entries show the media used by different companies, such as billboards, car cards, newspapers, magazines, advertising expenditures for each type, what accounts are handled by different agencies. All in all, through this service, an informative resumé of industry may be obtained.

Thomas' Register of American Manufacturers, that massive green volume familiar to industry, is another over-all compendium of manufacturing distribution. Its breakdown by type of industry is an avenue to production information in many lines. Its alphabetical listing of companies provides a guide to the location of a manufacturer whose name, but not address, is known. Its trade name index is a boon.

Thomas' Register is probably the most consulted buying guide in the United States. In its introduction it states that its aim "is to include all manufacturers, producers, and all other similar sources of supply in all lines in all parts of the United States, except such as cater to restricted local trade only." The two principal volumes are a classified listing of products, subdivided according to localities, in alphabetical arrangement. As an example, the classification "Pumps, Hand," begins with a manufacturer in California: Burbank, and ends with one in Wisconsin: Superior.

To use *Thomas' Register* intelligently, the "Index" or "Product Finding Guide" should be consulted. This alone is a revelation of the scope of American manufacturing. For example, buttons are classified under 57 subdivisions, and pins under 128. Cross references in the index are excellent and may have special interest such as the reference from "crocodile shears" to "machinery: shearing alligator."

Volume III of *Thomas' Register* has an A-Z listing of American manufacturers, with addresses of home, branch offices, and subsidiaries, some indication of their capitalization, and partial list of products. It has also a list of commerce associations, trade papers, and brand names.

Although intended primarily as a buying guide for industry and business, *Thomas' Register* is particularly valuable in locating the manufacturers of unusual products, and it is safe to say, "If it's made in America, *Thomas'* will tell who makes it and where." Wood flour, prefabricated houses, hand warmers, wicker pony carts, velours for powder puffs, fox food, soft capsules filled with gelatin, and feather dusters are only a few of the items seldom found through ordinary merchandising channels, but whose makers are listed in *Thomas' Register.* The volume should be examined at least once by anyone with more than a passing interest in the American business scene.

Kelly's *Directory of Merchants, Manufacturers and Shippers* is another long-established publication listing by countries and cities the manufacturers and chief industrialists in all trades. That essential guide, an international alphabetical listing of firms, is found in the *International Register.* Primarily a cable guide, it gives also companies by types of industry and is particularly valuable as a guide to business firms throughout the world.

A typical trade directory supplement to a periodical is the annual directory number of *Hardware Age,* which is a directory for the hardware trade. This issue may contain 20,000 brand names of products as well as the names of more than 10,000 products and 60,000 manufacturers. A directory which aims to be an authoritative reference book for the whole industry is the *Petroleum Register.* It gives the history, capital structure, personnel, location, and production capacity of both refineries and manufacturing plants. It discusses market facilities and areas of distribution, lists trade associations and government bureaus, indexes foreign oil companies and refineries, and gives a five-year survey of the finances of United States oil companies.

DIRECTORIES AS AIDS IN IDENTIFYING TRADEMARKS

Identification of trademarks and trade names is an important phase of business research. According to the *Standard Advertising Register,* there are over 500,000 trade names in use in the United States, and over 125,000 of these are registered. In selection of a trade name, sources must be checked to determine prior use or similarity in sound and spelling. Frequently legal advice is employed in making extensive searches involved in establishing and registering a trade name, but the preliminary investigation in directories may be made by the producer or processor himself.

Frequently, a brand name is the only clue to the name of the manufacturer. Advertising in newspapers and magazines and through radio and television has made many brand names such as

"Victrola," "Dynaflow," and "Tootsie Roll" parts of everyday language, but at the same time buried the name of the manufacturer. The daily avalanche of advertising has increased the use of available lists which link the address of the producer with his product.

It was to fill such a gap in business information that the Science-Technology Group of the Special Libraries Association, with the help of the Technology Department of the Carnegie Library of Pittsburgh, compiled a *Trade-Names Index.* The sponsors of this publication made no effort to include registered trademarks published by the United States Patent Office. The list is concerned more with definitions of materials, processes, and technical equipment. A useful feature of this carefully assembled work is a classified bibliography of sources for trade names, trademarks, and brand names. This furnishes additional sources to be searched for trade names not on readily available lists.

Thomas' Register in Volume III has "The American Trade Name Index," which it describes as "the buyer's quick reference list of leading trade names, special brands, etc., under which various products are stamped, labeled, and advertised, etc." As a supplementary service available through correspondence, the Thomas Publishing Company maintains a file of inactive trade names. Another source of brand name indentification is MacRae's *Blue Book,* a classified buyers' guide to American manufactured products.

Trade directories sometimes list brand names. One of these is *Chemical Week Buyer's Guide,* the annual directory number of that magazine. This publishes brand names for chemicals, raw materials, specialties, equipment, and container products. Another example is *Variety Stores Merchandiser Directory* of *Variety Market,* which lists brand names of novelty store items. Trade catalogs should always be considered in any search for brand name identification. The *Standard Advertising Register* has a comprehensive list of the better-known trade names used by national advertisers.

VARIED USES OF THE CITY DIRECTORY

City directories have been published in this country since 1785. The first city directories gave little information. Now they provide not only a variety of data in the alphabetical section, but also record street locations, state, country, city, and federal data, the statistical record of the city, and other information vital in forming a reliable estimate of a community.

The city directory may be used as a key to an understanding of its development. Frequently it includes condensed information on population, industry, public utilities, government agencies, ratables, and tax rates. This and other similar information can be compared over a period of years to discover trends in development. More extensive information about the city's industrial growth and shifts in area use can be secured by comparative treatment of facts shown in the classified and street sections.

In a typical city directory a section may include a list of governmental officers of the city, the county, the state, and the country. A classified section under the various headings such as banks, barbers, tailors, lawyers, real estate agents, etc., provides an inclusive survey of the business activities of the communities covered. Usually this section contains names of associations, groups, and societies, with some specific information about their meetings, and of churches and their clergy. The alphabetical section indicates the name, address, and profession of those listed, with occasional additional information. The numerical section, included in many directories, contains a list of street names and locations and a list of residents by street numbers. Symbols are used to indicate telephone subscribers and home owners.

The Newark volume, published by Price and Lee, is an excellent example of the best type of city directory. Exceptionally full information about individuals facilitates identification. From its pages it is possible to tell the number of telephones in a given area, the property owners, the number of married people, and types of occupation most prevalent in given sections. The value and usefulness of a really adequate city directory as a sociological agent has not yet been fully sensed. Its immediate value in gauging a city's potential market is apparent.

Publication of a city directory is feasible only where a sufficient number of advertisers will find purchase of space profitable, and so underwrite the major cost of the enterprise. In the case of cities such as New York and Chicago, the cost of assembling directory information is prohibitive.

In heavily populated areas the telephone directory must be the chief reliance for local information. It does not supersede the city directory, since it is concerned with telephone subscribers only, and as a rule only one name for each telephone. It does, however, meet many needs when no recent city directory is available. The classified section, usually incorporated with the telephone directory, is of even more importance for business use than the directory itself. In special cases, notably in Chicago and New York, the Classified section is published by a separate corporation such as the Reuben H. Donnelley Corporation, and under certain restrictions, is provided to telephone subscribers as a supplementary service. No one in business in these cities could afford to be without one, and they are used extensively by out-of-town buyers and sellers.

The various directories described above are must publications for an adequate library collection. Less important but useful are the infrequently published state gazetteers or general directories of selected business concerns, and the regional directories, such as the *Directory of New England Manufacturers.*

chapter VI

The Government-Federal and State Information Reservoirs

The government as a source of business data. Channels for government information. Applications of government data to business problems. Information on government purchasing. Sources of information about government publications. Securing government publications. State publications for business use. State industrial directories.

THE GOVERNMENT AS A SOURCE OF BUSINESS DATA

The American businessman is fortunate to have at his command, through the federal government, the world's greatest reservoir and dispenser of statistical information. Responsive to the demands of its citizens and conscious of the practical value of experience records, the government has traditionally published authoritative data for the businessman. Nor is such statistical data all that is available to him. The government has sponsored economic studies of areas in this country and abroad, surveys of marketing practices in different types of business; reports on shifting population and industrial trends, all of which are at his disposal as a result of many cooperative activities between business groups and government institutions. Most of the material is in printed form, much more may be obtained through correspondence, while supplementing all these are the various counseling services reached through the regional offices of the Department of Commerce. So, through the businessman's cooperation, a picture of the American business scene and its many areas and subdivisions has been drawn, which as a basis of comparison with his individual enterprise, may be a challenge and a guide to each executive.

Because government functions must be interpreted in order to be effective, the voluminous accumulation of statistical and historical material in its published form, placed the government in first position as the world's largest publisher. Some idea of the range and extent of these publications may be obtained by a glance at the multitude of price lists issued by the Superintendent of Documents. In approaching an understanding of the reservoir of information it should be kept in mind that there are two general divisions. One comprises the documents that bear on the record of legislative proceedings, the laws, the manuals of procedure, and the official directories. The other, the more fruitful for general use, is made up of the publications that stem from research by government agencies.

From this wealth of material bearing upon education, health, history, science, and other phases of national life, the government's service in compiling business data emerges as the chief factor in developing the exchange of information that has so influenced the growth of American industry. Both business and government, as a matter of fact, have needed statistical records. Such important arms of the national government as the Bureau of the Census, the Bureau of Foreign and Domestic Commerce, the Bureau of Labor Statistics, the Office of Business Economics, the Bureau of Agricultural Economics, the Business and Defense Services Administration, the United States Tariff Commission, the Federal Trade Commission, the Board of Governors of the Federal Reserve System are high among the numerous agencies that have compiled data of daily use in business activities. Years of cooperation between government units, trade associations, schools of business, research bodies, labor unions, and other groups have gone into this development of statistical data and information on business conditions and practice. Through the government's machinery for assembling, compiling, and distributing information, these data are returned for business use.

CHANNELS FOR GOVERNMENT INFORMATION

The channels through which the government returns this compiled information as a measuring instrument for business progress vary from publication of such periodicals as the *Survey of Current Business* to the long files of census volumes or the various periodic issues in the Foreign Trade series of the Census Bureau. The standard reference books such as the *Statistical Abstract of the United States, 1789-1945, the County and City Data Book, 1952,* the directories such as the *Official Postal Guide,* the statistical compilations outlined in *Statistical Services of the United States Government,* the special files of material supplemented regularly dealing with such subjects as *Management Aids for the Small Business* furnished by the Small Business Administration, all illustrate these channels of distribution.

Because of the inclusive nature of government publications, the businessman who wishes to make the most efficient use of these resources should endeavor to take two steps. The first is to acquire a broad general knowledge of the departments, their publications, and the statistical features of their major activities. The second is to select the several publications that seem of immediate use and to become familiar with the data they contain. In accomplishing this the local public library can be of assistance. These institutions have extensive collections of such publications. A visit to their shelves and collections will enable any inquirer to use experienced observation in making his selection of publications for his own purchase.

An invaluable guide in discovering the statistical series most useful in a particular business is *Government Statistics for Business Use* by P. M. Hauser and W. R. Leonard. A study of this volume in the light of his personal needs will do much to enable the businessman to select publications that should receive his consistent attention. A comprehensive list geared to business needs and useful as a guide in the selection of business literature is the *Business Service Checklist,* a weekly list of material made available by the Department of Commerce. Still another publication is "*Popular Guide to Government Publications,*" which presents selected titles of government publications in diversified subjects, together with a synopsis of their contents.

In forming an idea of the functions and possible publications of the different divisions of the government, the *United States Government Organization Manual* is a basic guide. This official handbook describes every agency of the legislative, executive, and judicial branches, and includes sections relating to quasi-official agencies.

The Department of Commerce is the main agency for providing materials useful in the general business program. Among its publications those of the Bureau of Census are valuable for the background of business data they furnish through the statistical compilations based on census studies and other reports. Chief among these are the *Census of Manufactures,* the *Census of Business,* the population studies, the reports on retail store sales, the foreign trade summaries, and the bulletins on purchasing power of families and income and rent available through the Census of Housing. The *County Business Patterns* books of the Census Bureau give pertinent information on manufacturing employment.

Besides these reports, the Department of Commerce and the Small Business Administration are responsible for an expanding series of studies of business management and details of operation. Much of this material is made available through special publications. Additional data and case studies appear in the *Small Business Aids* pamphlets. The Office of Technical Services of the Commerce Department offers an extremely valuable and often overlooked source of information of practical use in manufacturing and other businesses.

It supplies at nominal cost a quantity of scientific and technical information arising mainly from the government's annual investment of more than $2 billion a year in research and development. This information is contained in some 250,000 reports bearing directly or indirectly on development of new or improved products and processes. Thousands of these reports are on sale by the Office of Technical Services in printed form, and the remainder by the Library of Congress in microfilm or photocopy form. New reports are abstracted in the OTS's monthly *U.S. Government Research Reports* (formerly *Bibliography of Technical Reports*). Existing reports are listed by category in the numerous *Catalogs of Technical Reports.* For many firms, especially smaller ones without research facilities, these reports have proved a gold mine of ideas and technical help.

Manufacturers seeking generalized aid in determining suitable products for their facilities have found *Developing and Selling New Products* a valuable guide. The 1954 revision of this book is scheduled for early publication jointly by OTS and the Small Business Administration.

The Bureau of Labor Statistics of the Department of Labor is another government agency to which business looks for valuable data. Many statistical series are compiled through this office that have immediate bearing on wage negotiations and other employment problems. Chief among these are the series on cost of living, retail prices, wage rates, man hours, labor turnover, and similar topics. A detailed discussion of such data, with particular reference to the New York metropolitan area appeared in *Business Literature* for November 1946.

Among the publications and activities of the Department of Agriculture that have a direct bearing on general business enterprise are the reports on the economic status of the farm as an industrial enterprise. Of these, the greater number are compiled and issued by the Bureau of Agricultural Economics and the Production and Marketing Administration. These reports deal with crops and markets, agricultural prices, the farm income situation, marketing, transportation, and family spending and saving in wartime, and are a direct reflection of the economic status of a basic industry.

Several other federal agencies publish reports and studies of particular value to business. Among these the Federal Trade Commission has issued industry-wide studies on profits such as its comprehensive survey of chain store activities. This includes data on prices, margin, sales, costs, and profits. Another intermittent publisher of monographs is the Tariff Commission. This agency has made analytical studies on foreign trade with special emphasis on United States imports and exports.

Other publications providing exhaustive financial surveys on a range of subjects from corporation statistics to installment sales are issued by the Securities and Exchange Commission and the Board of Governors of the Federal Reserve System. Nor can the report to the President by the Council of Economic Advisors be overlooked in any consideration of recommended business reading.

Another source of specialized information peculiar to the American system is to be found in the published reports of public hearings before congressional committees. At these hearings organizations or individuals may appear and present evidence in support of their views on legislation being considered by the committee, or on matters of public concern under investigation. This frequently means inclusion of much relevant factual data. For example, the Temporary National Economic Committee was authorized to make "full study and investigation with respect to concentration of economic power in, and financial control over production and distribution of goods and services." This committee worked intensively on its assignment, and its many volumes of hearings and the monographs comprising studies made by different agencies for this committee bring together an unprecedented collection of economic data. The reports of the hearings themselves, while rather difficult to use because of the nature of the proceedings, include the testimony of experts and are supplemented by innumerable charts and tables. While some hearings are unusual in the extent of material adduced, any hearing in relation to business problems will have useful supplemental data.

Although the divergent demands brought about by specific business problems are such that no one list can be the universal answer, the range of information is so wide in the various distributed publications that they serve as their own guide to their possible usefulness. An aid in their selection will be the examination of illustrative publications at the public library. The October to December 1950 issues of *Business Literature* contain descriptive lists of government publications of special value to business and include references to other checklists and handbooks.

APPLICATIONS OF GOVERNMENT DATA TO BUSINESS PROBLEMS

In any consideration of the most effective use of government statistical series a careful study of *Government Statistics for Business Use* by P. M. Hauser and W. R. Leonard is a recommended first step. In this, the descriptions of the compilation and coverage of the various data are ably reinforced by accounts of their application to the immediate business problems of both the small and the large operator. These records of statistics of retail sales, farm income, and population shifts may be a familiar story to market research experts and other students of statistical data, but even familiar processes are given suggestive treatment in the course of these discussions. The value of farm income reports as a basis for estimating possible markets for farm equipment is well known. Too, national averages in production and other phases of particular industries are recognized as standards of measurement that must be surpassed if individual businesses are to become successful. But the illustration of the study of the number of incubators in a given area as a basis for deciding on the possible market for coal, may carry suggestion for similar uses in different fields. It is in the variety of applications and the detail of the discussion that this study is most enlightening.

In the operation of almost any phase of business the management will find information of value in the publications of the Department of Commerce. The extent of this information is indicated through the use which can be made of some publications in the domain of foreign trade. Here the first approach may well be through the pages of *Guides for New World Traders,* a publication of the Office of International Trade, under revision by its successor agency, the Bureau of Foreign Commerce. This compact pamphlet discusses the broad aspect of world trade, indicates some of the major problems and their solution, and what is even more important, guides the reader to additional sources of information. *Channels of Trading Abroad* is also a concise guide for the businessman concerned with foreign trade. Along with examination of this publication, regular reference to *Foreign Commerce Weekly* with its news by countries, and regular reports on exchange rates, new world trade leads, and other current items is called for. Supplementing the *Weekly*'s news reports is the new *World Trade Information Service,* offering additional or more detailed information.

Two publications of special value to the exporter are *Modern Export Packing* and *Modern Ship Stowage.* These cover such essential details as the sizes of containers, packing for various commodities, weighing the problem of custom charges. Points about parcel post and express shipment and protection in transit are all discussed. *Ship Stowage* gives detail in connection with cargo handling, loading and unloading, storage to prevent damage of all kinds, instructions for special cargoes, and essential notes on terms, weights, and measures. Of direct utility to businessmen seeking outlets or sources of supply abroad are the *Trade Lists,* which are listings of foreign firms and individuals by type of activity and by country. These can be purchased through the field office of the Department of Commerce.

In understanding economic factors affecting specific countries the *Foreign Commerce Yearbook* has been a valuable guide. Last issued for 1951, it gives facts about each nation with respect to area and population, principal crops and production, transportation detail, foreign trade, imports and exports of principal commodities, trade with principal countries, and trade with the United States by principal commodities for a series of comparable years. Even more detailed information of general value to traders is contained in a series of guidebooks on the conditions and outlook for United States investors in foreign countries. These books, published by the Bureau of Foreign Commerce, include volumes on Colombia, Venezuela, India, Pakistan, and the Union of South Africa.

In considering possible contacts for developing the export market, two other publications warrant attention. *Channels for Trading Abroad* provides information about channels through which goods may be imported or exported and indicates methods by which representatives abroad may be found. *Foreign Trade Associations in the United States* supplements this by listing the more than 700 business and cultural associations having a special interest in foreign countries' affairs. These publications and many others touching on different aspects or more detailed subdivisions of foreign trade afford American businessmen the opportunity to put to work for profit the information for many spheres of activity compiled by government agencies.

INFORMATION ON GOVERNMENT PURCHASING

The emergence of Uncle Sam as the businessman's best customer has increased the importance of two publications containing federal procurement news. The most important of these is the *Synopsis of Proposed Procurements and Contracts Awards Information,* compiled daily and issued by the Field Service of the U.S. Department of Commerce. The other is the *U.S. Government Advertiser.*

Few people realize the magnitude of government purchases. With the realization that such demands on the nation's industrial resources can be met only by encouraging private enterprise to work with the government, there has been a concerted effort to create conditions of fair and direct dealing between the government and the businessman. One step in cutting the "red tape" so dreaded by the businessman has been unification of procurement policies of all the branches of the armed services and consolidation of Army and Navy purchasing offices.

The *Synopsis of Proposed Procurements and Contracts Awards Information* lists proposed procurements issued by the various U.S. Government procurement offices, and the alert businessman who follows this publication will learn of extensive markets for both services and materials, which may include enlarging a post office in California, furnishing steel chairs for an atomic energy installation in Idaho, 1,700,000 cups of assorted flavored ice cream for a South Carolina Army camp, and orders exceeding $250,000 worth of rayon twill cloth for the New York Quartermaster Procurement Agency. This publication frequently also includes advance announcement of surplus property sales by military and civilian government agencies. It is available on subscription.

The *U.S. Government Advertiser,* established in 1882 and published every Thursday, also gives detailed information about federal procurement. This publication has alphabetical lists of products the government wants to buy and of agencies making purchases. It also records "invitations to bid," and the bidder on a contract can learn in its Bids and Awards columns what the competition bid and who got the award. The listings include both defense and non-defense contracts. This newspaper also has brief news items of interest to the government contractor.

Additional information on procurement in connection with government programs for economic recovery in foreign countries is found in the publications of the Foreign Operations Administration. This federal agency on December 30, 1951 assumed the functions and responsibilities of the Economic Cooperation Administration. The Office of Small Business of the Foreign Operations Administration also issues publications containing general information on doing business with foreign countries and listing specific economic needs abroad.

SOURCES OF INFORMATION ABOUT GOVERNMENT PUBLICATIONS

The government itself through the *Price Lists, United States Government Publications Monthly Catalog, Business Service Check List,* of the Department of Commerce, that Department's cumulative catalog and index, and other publications, is the chief source of information. The *Distribution Data Guide,* issued monthly by the Business and Defense Services Administration of the Department of Commerce, cites current governments as well as private publications, articles, and reports which bear on marketing.

Discussion of government publications and their use has appeared in various nongovernmental publications also. Of these, the most comprehensive and adaptable from the business point of view is *Government Statistics for Business Use* by P. M. Hauser and W. R. Leonard. While limited to discussion of statistical data in its treatment of subjects, it provides a broad range for research from national income, manufacturing, agriculture, wholesale, retail, and international trade, to money, credit and banking, population, housing, and labor. Not only descriptions of the statistical materials, but stimulating discussion of their application to details of business management are included. All in all this book is essential for the businessman interested in getting the best information return on his support of the federal government.

Government Publications and Their Use by Laurence F. Schmeckebier is a more general treatment with special attention to administration publications such as bills, federal laws, and court decisions. Though limited in its use for business in contrast to the Hauser book, the chapter on maps, as one of the few detailed discussions of this subject available, is of special value.

Two books, primarily intended as library aids in handling and using these publications are *Subject Guide to the United States Government Publications* by H. S. Hirschberg and C. C. Melinat, and *United States Government Publications* by Anne Morris Boyd. The first is a descriptive list of publications by subject. The references under such business headings as advertising, airports, bankruptcy, banks, and banking, building industry, business, and so on down the line make the book a profitable one for consultation at the public library. The second, *United States Government Publications,* is a thorough study arranged by departmental publication.

Business Literature frequently lists and describes government publications in connection with the various topics, banking, real estate, foreign trade, covered in its monthly issues. Recent numbers have stressed the relations between business and government. "Put Your Business House in Order," May 1947, was devoted to the Department of Commerce publications for small business. "Business Observers for Federal Activities" in the January 1947 issue, while not limited to government publications, emphasizes the reports in various forms covering the government coming out of Washington.

SECURING GOVERNMENT PUBLICATIONS

The most direct way to obtain government publications is to order them through the Superintendent of Documents. The price lists issued from that office give the necessary descriptions and terms. On occasion, the answer to a request for information addressed to the various departments will be supplemented by some government publication. To some extent congressmen may draw on these resources for their constituents. The increasing number of requests for different government items from businessmen is an indication that these government services are making a direct return to the citizen.

All public libraries have collections of government publications. Because these publications cover different phases of business activity and from so many points of view, a practical step in choosing the most appropriate is to examine those in the local library collection. In the many regional offices of the Department of Commerce are publications both for sale or for examination. The extent to which these regional offices may be a potential asset to business is all too little realized. Through his business organization and by telephone, visit, or by letter, the businessman may call on limitless government publication resources for the data by which he may improve his own opportunities.

STATE PUBLICATIONS FOR BUSINESS USE

While businessmen are aware to some extent of the wealth of economic material compiled by the federal government, and helpful to business enterprise, their knowledge of the extensive business information available from state and local governments is more limited. The growing influence of the state governments as agencies promoting human welfare has increased the number of state and local publications. Much of this information has accumulated as by-products of such administrative functions as unemployment relief, highway construction, regulation of public utilities, and conservation of natural resources.

Statistics of motor vehicle registration, employment trends, tax collections, and public school attendance are figures useful to the salesman. State departments of agriculture and employment have long lists of publications which may include market news on truck gardening, weekly reports on the livestock market, the state farm census, and summaries of earnings and hours worked by industry.

Other state publications are especially useful as informative sources for the directors of a business enterprise, either starting or expanding operations in new territories. Of particular interest is the *Small Business Series* of the New York State Department of Commerce. Many state and local government publications are free. Excellent gratis material may include maps. For example, airport, railroad, and town-and-country maps may be obtained free from the New York State Department of Commerce.

A comprehensive listing of the publications of state and local governments is contained in Part II of *Market Research Sources 1950,* ninth edition, published by the United States Department of Commerce. The authoritative source of state publication is the *Monthly Checklist of State Publications,* which is sold by the Superintendent of Documents, Government Printing Office in Washington. This checklist records state documents received by the Library of Congress. The easiest method for obtaining state publications is to apply for them directly to the state or local government which issues them. The seeker after business data who can force upon himself an acquaintance with these severe-looking and unadorned lists of government publications will be well rewarded by the discovery of extensive fields of business information which are accurate, up-to-date, and inexpensive.

STATE INDUSTRIAL DIRECTORIES

Invaluable sources of business data on the individual states are found in their industrial directories. These compact guides are varied in the kinds of information they include. The publication of these directories is often sponsored by such groups as the State Chamber of Commerce, the Bureau of Business Research of the state university, or the State Industrial Development Commission. All have the same purpose—to provide an accurate picture of the state's industrial development, which will serve as a guide to further business expansion. While publication may be at irregular intervals, new editions are frequent enough for up-to-date information.

The *New Jersey Industrial Directory,* published by the *Hudson Dispatch* of Union City, has general economic information about New Jersey, and statistical and other factual data about each borough, as well as a map of each county with accompanying description. The *Arizona Industrial Buyers' Guide,* issued by the Chamber of Commerce, Phoenix, lists wholesale distributors, as well as manufacturers. The *Directory of Florida Industries,* published by the Florida State Chamber of Commerce, Jacksonville, has summaries of Florida tax and corporate laws.

An outstanding illustration of regional directories is the *Directory of New England Manufacturers.* Not only has this directory alphabetical, geographical, and products sections, but it has a listing of brand and registered trademark names used by New England manufacturers. Along with this information the volume contains the addresses of defense agency officers in New England, members of Congress, names of societies, and condensed statistical data on the industrial growth of the region. It well fulfills its aim of "helping faraway places do business with New England."

The March 1952 issue of *Business Literature,* the monthly note of the Business Branch of the Public Library of Newark, New Jersey, is a descriptive list of state industrial directories which should be useful to both students of business and concerns operating over a large territory. According to this bibliography every state except Nevada, North Dakota, and Utah is represented by some kind of directory of its industries.

chapter VII

Associations and Business Progress

The contribution of business and trade associations. Predominating activities. Some noteworthy associations and their objectives. Sources of information about business and trade association programs.

THE CONTRIBUTION OF BUSINESS AND TRADE ASSOCIATIONS

Because industry in the United States early saw the value of cooperation, trade associations and business organizations have been formed by the hundred. Although in some industries they have served as a protective alliance, the main point for the purpose of the book is that they provide a channel for exchange of ideas. Thoughtful men and women, it is true, have looked upon business associations with mixed feelings for some years. As a matter of fact, in the past, many of these groups have been greatly censured for their policies and public relations. In recent years, as more progressive leadership has evolved, the constructive efforts of their organizations to secure adequate statistical reporting, conduct cost studies, develop employee training programs, and in general, provide better business information for their members' use have been of great benefit. The history of American business affords many illustrations of both wise and unwise association activities. But the changing times and the greater development of realism have brought a wider acceptance of the fact that sound business development is based not only on industrial profits, but also on community and national well-being.

Research organizations that are closely allied to business interests and whose work can be followed with profit are the National Bureau of Economic Research, the Brookings Institution, and the Twentieth Century Fund. While their approach is likely to be more along the lines of general research rather than consideration of a particular business problem, the results such as disclosed in *America's Needs and Resources,* issued by the Twentieth Century Fund, are of marked benefit in practical business planning. The American Management Association and the National Industrial Conference Board are other research associations dealing with business management problems. Supported by the leading corporations of the country, both associations have personnel of high caliber, and their studies are based on careful preparation and intensive analysis. When due recognition is given the sponsorship under which they are prepared, a high value may be attached to their many studies.

The more general type of business associations is represented by the Chamber of Commerce of the United States, and the National Association of Manufacturers. Without holding a brief for all the acts of these organizations, it may be said that departments in each have done noteworthy work in the newer spirit of research and analysis, and that wider recognition of consumer and labor relations have resulted in activities of progressive import.

The National Association of Manufacturers has announced that it aims to be the clearing house of information not only for its 15,000 members, but also for those in related industries such as suppliers of raw materials, distributors, and service trades. This organization, with headquarters in New York, has over 350 affiliated groups, and its numerous committees investigate and make recommendations on such controversial business issues as pending legislations, labor-management, and taxation.

The Chamber of Commerce of the United States is the largest over-all organization representing American business. With national headquarters in Washington, the membership includes nearly 2300 local chambers of commerce, 540 national and local trade associations, and 20,000 individual members. The Washington office of this organization prepares material of a general economic nature for use in individual business, either free or sold for a nominal sum.

Trade associations such as the National Paint, Varnish and Lacquer Association, the National Association of Dyers and Cleaners, the Edison Electric Institute, the Associated Business Papers, or the American Gas Association attempt to solve the problems common to their own industry. Many of the strong and conspicuous associations have done much for research in industry, in the development of better public relations, and for the promotion of efficient business methods. Illustrations of such activities are the research studies made possible by the Portland Cement Fellowship at the National Bureau of Standards of the Department of Commerce, the National Fertilizer Association's cooperation with state agricultural experiment stations, and the Southern Pine Association's wartime cooperation with the Army and Navy in a public relations program to stimulate lumber production. Another type of cooperation consists in providing business data to be used as public information or in compilations issued by the federal government, such as the statistical reports on production of ingots and steel by the American Iron and Steel Institute, the insurance sales by states and regions compiled by the Life Insurance Agency Management Association, or the weekly reports of electrical output and the monthly status of the electrical industry issued by the Edison Electric Institute.

The value of a study of its trade association in the investigation of a particular industry is great. Trade association publications reveal prevailing policies and practices. Not only is the public policy of the industry and its leaders implicit in association publications; the programs that have been carried out or inaugurated are an index to the industry's development. Consideration of the association's statistical records, of its work for education and research, and other progressive policies is useful in evaluating opportunities. Anyone already occupied in the industry will find work with his trade association may be one of the most stimulating features of his industrial career. As each member makes his association contact effective, and cooperates in developing a sound program, so does his own activity benefit. Such cooperation has been a major factor in contributing to industrial information and making it more widely available.

PREDOMINATING ACTIVITIES

The main purpose of trade associations has been to assist their members in dealing with mutual business problems, and their publications are intended primarily for members. With the development of a scientific approach to business in the effort to determine the causes of its basic variability, an increasing share of association budgets is being spent on economic research of a general nature. In recent years trade associations have sponsored studies on wages and hours, surveys on cost and cost accounting, and research on methods of hiring, training, promoting, and pensioning employees. As a result, many of their publications are now of interest to those in related trades as well as to the general public. They have printed extensive information on all phases of management-employee problems.

The possibilities for constructive action in trade associations are limitless. Through united effort, they may carry on research economically and profitably for the industry as a whole. Association publications may foster sound management, constructive public relations, wise cooperation with the government and with labor groups, and in other ways promote progressive business programs. By the same methods, they may, according to the quality of their leadership, make or mar these relations.

Foremost, perhaps, among the activities of a trade association is its service as a channel for information, especially through the annual conferences. Many associations publish bulletins, some of which have become the leading periodicals of a particular field. *Banking*, published by the American Bankers Association; *Credit and Financial Management*, issued by the National Association of Credit Men; *Journal of Accountancy*, published by the American Institute of Accountancy; all are examples of such leadership. Many of these publications with wide business circulation are supplemented by informal bulletins for members only.

Among the most useful publications of associations are their trade directories, which give information regarding sources of supply for the trade. These useful volumes are valuable not only as guides to the purchasing agent, salesman, advertiser, and processor, but as sources of information, in both its wholesale and retail aspects, about current conditions in the industry.

One of the chief ways in which the cooperative efforts of trade associations has led to improved methods is in the evolution of standards for products. Here the American Standards Association, largely an organization of technical and trade associations, has been instrumental in formulating standards and specifications to eliminate bottlenecks in industry. Another association carrying on a definite program of this type is the National Federation of Textiles, which has cooperated with the National Bureau of Standards in establishing methods of testing weighted silk and in considering specifications for standards in woven fabrics. This same cooperation was shown by the Society of the Plastic Industry in its work with the American Society for Testing Materials, the Federal Specifications Executive Committee, and the National Bureau of Standards during the war.

Cooperative effort by trade associations in developing sales programs has been another constructive activity. According to authoritative sources, the Edison Electric Institute and the National Electrical Wholesale Association, in cooperation with other associations in the industry, spent $150,000 to launch a sales training course. With this as the central feature, stress has been laid on scientific selection of sales personnel and adequate supervision of salesmen. In cooperation with the Business Education Service of the United States Office of Education, the National Paint, Varnish and Lacquer Association established a sales training course, and to provide a basis for classes, completed two texts, *Paint Power and How to Sell It* and a teacher's manual. A program based on home study was instituted by the American Dental Trade Association, which distributed volumes covering sales practice, sales and service, merchandise, sales conferences, and teeth and dental equipment.

United trade association effort in public relations represents another constructive activity. The safety program of the Pennsylvania Automotive Association, which included the appointment of a nationally known safety director, the development of programs involving dealer cooperation in traffic safety activities on the local level, and close cooperation in the administration and enforcement of the Motor Vehicle Inspection Law is an illustration of one such effort. The Ohio Association of Retail Lumber Dealers carried out another form of project when it financed, built, and exhibited a model farmstead at the Ohio State Fair so as to demonstrate to farmers a practical low-cost house and barn plan that would encourage them to build or remodel.

In connection with its over-all study, the Temporary National Economic Committee in 1941 issued *Monograph No. 18, Trade Association Survey,* an analysis of the characteristics and activities of trade associations at that time. This included extensive discussion of the methods used by various associations in compiling and disseminating statistical and other information. The study is supplemented by many tables and exhibits. While the information contained is not current, it is possibly the most comprehensive compilation of association information available. A list of trade associations classified by industry is included.

SOME NOTEWORTHY ASSOCIATIONS AND THEIR OBJECTIVES

Among general business groups rather than trade associations, the work of the Committee for Economic Development has been outstanding in maintaining high standards and concerted efforts to promote planning along economic lines. This organization of business leaders was formed in 1942 for two purposes: one, to stimulate country-wide postwar planning on the part of industry so as to offset the economic losses involved in the shift from wartime to peacetime operations; the other, through cooperative research by industrialists and economists to attempt to find an answer to some of the underlying economic problems of the day. This effort, with its related discussion in the press, was markedly successful in attaining the first objective through its emphasis on two steps: analysis of the individual business and use of business information in print. Its series of publications, compiled with the cooperation of many other associations, and illustrated by *Plan Postwar Jobs—Now,* published in 1943, did much to stimulate this business self-analysis. Its emphasis on the use of business information resources was illustrated by special publications and leaflets to strengthen library programs in service to business and industry.

The continuing effort of CED in the field of economic research has resulted in a number of noteworthy volumes such as *The Liquidation of War Production* by A. D. H. Kaplan, *Production, Jobs and Taxes* by Harold M. Graves, *International Trade and Domestic Employment* by Calvin B. Hoover, and *Agriculture in an Unstable Economy* by Theodore W. Schultz. Not only has CED contributed through research by competent economists, it has also recognized the place of the public library in bringing economic research to the grass roots.

In the American Management Association, business and industry have had for many years an organization that through research and the conference method has sought the answers to many problems with special emphasis on the field of personnel. Both the leaders of industry and expert consultants have participated in the association's efforts. A comprehensive publication program has permitted wide distribution of the papers presented at its conferences on marketing, production, financial, personnel, and office management. Through a special membership, the various publications are made generally available. They have long been the main reliance of investigation in these subject fields. Another association contribution, the publication of periodicals such as *Management Review* and *Personnel,* with their thoughtful articles and excellent book reviews, has been an educational influence in the field of management research.

Another joint effort of business and industry to find the facts on which to base plans is represented by the National Industrial Conference Board. This organization, with a board of directors drawn from leading industrialists, and staffed by economists, has since 1916 compiled studies on basic factors in business economics, business practices, and management research. Statistical series covering earnings and working conditions in manufacturing industries, clerical salary rates, consumer price indexes, measures of comparative living costs, are compiled regularly and published in detail in *The Conference Board Management Record.* For years its series of charts, *Road Maps of Industry,* discussing a variety of ecomonic trends, have been standards of graphic presentation of statistical changes or developments. Like the American Management Association, conference and round-table discussions are major activities, though in this instance economic and industrial policies rather than management phases are emphasized.

The numerous publications of the Conference Board in format, phraseology, and subject matter are designed to be particularly useful to the businessman. Their publications include an annual *Economic Almanac,* which they describe as a handbook of useful facts about business, labor, and government in the United States and other areas, a weekly one-page summary of changes in business indicators called *A Desk Sheet,* and two series called *Studies in Business Economics* and *Studies in Business Policy.* The Conference Board is supported by subscriptions for its publications and services from national and state business associations, business concerns, labor organizations, public institutions, and interested individuals.

Various other groups have done important work in basic studies. Notable among them in securing foundation as well as academic support are the National Bureau of Economic Research, the Brookings Institution, and the Twentieth Century Fund. The National Bureau of Economic Research has specialized in studies on business cycles, national income and wealth, and prices and pricing policies. It has to its credit many volumes on these subjects and other economic questions.

A primary purpose in the foundation of the Brookings Institution was to enable it to serve as an aid in development of sound national policies based on scientific research in the social sciences. These studies have been made generally available through publication. Among them have been one on the distribution of wealth and income in relation to economic progress, one on the factors responsible for stagnation in the American capital market, and one on relief and its administration. Publications have included *America's Capacity to Produce, America's Capacity to Consume, Income and Economic Progress, Capital Expansion, Employment and Economic Stability, Relief and Social Security, Guarantee of Annual Wages.*

The Twentieth Century Fund was founded and endowed to make scientific surveys of the facts underlying pressing economic problems as an aid in solving these problems. One of its earlier studies, *Financing the Consumer* by Evans Clark, grew out of the Fund's interest in the American credit union movement. Recent activities have had one chief goal—"rebuilding a sound and prosperous economic system after the strains and dislocations of the war." In one series, written by Stuart Chase, the Fund offered the public a provocative picture of some of the problems to be faced. In its comprehensive survey, *America's Needs and Resources*, Dr. J. Frederic Dewhurst and his associates have presented an estimate of America's human and industrial capacity and resources.

SOURCES OF INFORMATION ABOUT BUSINESS AND TRADE ASSOCIATION PROGRAMS

The American Trade Association Executives, with its headquarters in Washington, is the authoritative information source with respect to its members. The annual proceedings reflect their diversified interests. Its *Membership Directory* is a who's who of association management. Further information about trade associations may be found in the *American Trade Association Executives Journal* published quarterly by the Association. Its articles deal mostly with the legal aspects of trade association activities, policy making, and public relations. Special publications bring together the combined experience and observation of members in particular fields.

An authoritative listing of trade associations is *National Associations of the United States*, by Jay Judkins, Chief, Trade Association Division, Office of Domestic Commerce, and published by the U.S. Department of Commerce in 1949. Another Department of Commerce publication, the outdated but descriptive volume *Trade Association Activities*, provides a background for understanding the development of the whole movement.

Publications of regional chambers of commerce usually deal with industrial resources and economic development of the local area, and frequently are sources of local trade information which cannot be obtained elsewhere. Many of these organizations have libraries of their own. Usually they have information about new businesses in the area. They are excellent sources of data for those who are investigating plant location. Some issue publications describing advantages of the area. Their publications range from news bulletins and summaries of business activity to directories of local business and industrial concerns. *Market Research Sources*, 1950, 9th edition, published by the U.S. Department of Commerce, has a comprehensive listing of Chamber of Commerce publications dealing with marketing.

The constructive and effective role of the trade association in modern American industry has been thoroughly described in the well-documented and fully illustrated *How to Use Your Trade Association* by Walter Mitchell, Jr. The author was in the Department of Commerce during the presidency of Herbert Hoover. As Secretary of Commerce, Mr. Hoover realized that business groups were handicapped by lack of organization, and he was one of the first government officials to encourage formation of trade associations and call public attention to their possibilities. Later Mr. Mitchell was executive director of the Wool Institute, a trade association of wool textile manufacturers.

Among other sources, succinct but basic information on many business associations in fields that impinge upon and affect public administration is given in the descriptive listings found in *Public Administration Organizations: A Directory*. A more comprehensive but less descriptive list, arranged geographically, is included in *Public Relations Directory and Yearbook*. *Business Literature* for June 1945, in the article "Trade Associations as Sources of Information," carries an annotated list of publications on trade associations in general as well as a list of illustrative publications of these organizations.

chapter VIII

"Services"—The Answer to Special Information Needs

The why and what of services. Services in general. Illustrative services in special fields Uses of services. The field of the financial services. Advisory and forecasting services. Income tax and other loose-leaf services. Sources of information on services.

THE WHY AND WHAT OF SERVICES

As a result of conditions calling for specific types of information, "services" in variety have developed. These information media are, in general, publications that "supply information in easily usable form, not readily available otherwise." One of the earliest, *Poor's Manuals,* evolved from the investment needs of banks and other institutions for authentic information consistently maintained, on the financial structure of railroads. As interest in the affairs of large corporations broadened, so did the services increase in number and in the extent of their information coverage. In more recent years business has felt the need for data to serve specific, definite purposes; and this demand has been met by some expert compiler of information who has sensed the possible market. *Moody's, Kiplinger, Dodge Reports, Dun & Bradstreet* all familiar friends to the business world, are the results of a keen appreciation of the potentialities of such expert reporting.

Many services cover investments, law, government regulations, insurance, advertising, construction, commodities, and other interests. Important institutions such as Moody's or Standard & Poor's for investments, Best and Spectator for insurance reports, Commerce

Clearing House and Prentice-Hall for government and legal reporting, all have grown out of consumer needs. The reliability and effectiveness of their special publications can be judged by the success with which they have met the test of constant and immediate use by their subscribers.

SERVICES IN GENERAL

Services take many forms and are published under varying conditions. The famous and costly investment services include fat volumes of corporation reports, supplemented by weekly bulletins on changing conditions but consistent in the subject matter. The vital question of business conditions as affected by state and federal statutes has produced many services that focus attention and exhaustive legal study on these problems. Prentice-Hall, Commerce Clearing House, and National Research Institute are publishers that have brought skilled editorial attention to the subject. Data on tax questions and legal services in general are other contributions they have made in fields where specialized interpretation is essential. Since that factor of specialized interpretation cannot be overlooked, such services are treated in general terms only in this discussion of the information tools of business.

The "service" field is one in which organizations come and go. The histories of the best of these show that accurate and intelligent reporting, sound procedure, and close observation of a particular activity from the viewpoint of the specialist have brought rewards to their farsighted originators through the reliable and timesaving aids they have furnished business in all fields. A sound principle, therefore, in meeting a recurring need for business information is to determine first whether there exists a special "service" to meet that need.

ILLUSTRATIVE SERVICES IN SPECIAL FIELDS

Because of the increasing complexity of government business relations and the resulting necessity for a better understanding of the problems and opportunities involved in this relationship, various Washington news letters have come into being. Among these the *Kiplinger Washington Letter* is perhaps the most widely known.

Kiplinger is a compact four-page report on legislative and official activities. Its pointed observations on what goes on in governmental circles, frequently based on opinion surveys of informed business leadership, have proved their value over the years. The weekly receipt of this *Letter* is awaited with keen interest in many offices and by the regular frequenters of business libraries.

Another Washington service useful for its systematic and interpretative reporting on congressional developments is the *Congressional Quarterly,* which through weekly bulletins and quarterly cumulations enables the constituents of any legislator to follow his actions and progress as their representative in Congress. Services of this caliber are also of great value to today's businessman in the opportunity they offer for intelligent appraisal of legislative programs.

Construction and real estate are other fields where special needs have resulted in establishment of such services as *Brown's Letters, Real Estate Analyst, Housing Bulletin,* etc. The construction industry with its dependence on current developments has provided a market for such services as *Brown's Letters* and *Dodge Reports.* These meet a daily but ephemeral need and so consist only of stenciled sheets that give specific information about construction activities, bids wanted, and awards for building construction in the metropolitan areas. On the other hand, problems affecting construction and real estate in the long-range investment programs of insurance companies and other large investors call for compilation of many special statistical reports and analyses. Here *The Real Estate Analyst* provides a valuable aid with its appraisal studies, reports on mortgage trends, analyses of tax ranges in different areas, and reports on housing conditions. Still another service, important in relation to housing developments but simplified in its treatment, is the *Housing Letter,* particularly enlightening to the individual tenant, landlord, and real estate operator in a more limited field.

While the magazines devoting themselves to advertising, selling, and the various aspects of marketing satisfy in general the information needs of their readers, certain techniques have been developed by the publishers of services that make a more immediate and direct appeal in the realm of public and customer relations, sales, etc. A service of this type is *Dealer Relations and Sales Promotion Plans* issued by the Dartnell Corporation. For many years this company has devoted intensive effort to aiding the sales executive. The increasing attention being given to costs and special studies in the sales factors is reflected in their publications.

Public Relations News is another publication evolved to meet the concern with new methods of fostering mutual understanding of common interests. In its reporting of current methods for interpreting management to labor and vice versa, for making corporation problems and programs clear to stockholders, for integrating plant activities with community progress, it carries on a broad educational activity. Its comments on noteworthy publications in the field of public relations are useful as a guide to important items in the ever-swelling stream of business print.

USES OF SERVICES

The uses of services vary with the field of concentration and the interest of the reader. For example, the *Standard Advertising Register* is a listing of many firms and advertising agencies, as well as a geographical index to agencies and their accounts. But it may also be used as a key to much other information. The main volume is a list of national advertisers arranged by industry. The information for each company includes the names of officers, research directors, accountants, and others. It includes also the capitalization, the location, the advertising appropriation, the agency, the media used, and their distribution. Other volumes are concerned with advertising agencies and their accounts, with both a geographic and alphabetical listing. The information is kept up to date by supplementary lists during the year. Its value to the advertising agency is obvious. Collaterally it is valuable as a general source of information relative to business activity.

The *Standard Advertising Register* is primarily a selective list of leading companies in many fields, a key to a quality market. If a sampling of reactions to an idea, a product or a service by business leaders is sought, a list as comprehensive or selective as is desired may be easily assembled within a wide range of activity by use of the main volume. Should some gauge of the relative amounts spent for advertising in newspapers or on billboards be needed, the information there recorded on expenditures for different media will provide the basis for an estimate. Regional trends in industrial developments are often matters of serious consideration. Again a selective guide to such developments is found in *Standard Advertising*. To what extent has research as a definite organizational activity been recognized by industry and in what fields? Through thoughtful analysis, deductions may be drawn from the facts recorded there. For the established business executive wishing important general information on industrial subjects, the *Standard Advertising Register*, studied with discernment and imagination, can provide an inexhaustible supply of material. To the man seeking new and profitable connections, its pages show as many points of contacts. In addition to the *Standard Advertising Register*, *McKittrick's Directory of Advertisers* contains related information organized along different lines. Where geographic distribution is the major approach, *McKittrick* will be a timesaver, while *Standard* remains the immediate guide to leaders in specific industries regardless of location.

The annual statements condensed and assembled in the investment manuals and services published by Moody, Fitch, Standard & Poor's are well known for their evaluation of the financial position of the many companies reported. As interesting and enlightening to the market analyst and the sales manager are the weekly reports on changing conditions furnished by these and other companies. Industrial developments that indicate expanding markets for the sale of many products may be gauged through these reports. Decentralization or relocation of industries is reflected there. Employment changes, and the industries with greatest possibilities for expansion, may be deduced through the facts noted. The respective growths of individual companies and their policies in relation to current trends all may be read between the lines. Their major function, however, is the provision of investment information.

The primary function of the financial sources is to serve as an aid to the would-be investor. They provide information dealing with the trend of the stock and bond market, the outlook of specific industries and companies, and economic and financial data of government units. Since these services are excellent, the potential investor would be well advised to read several, then supplement this information with the data to be gained from a study of the various investment journals and the annual reports of the companies under consideration.

THE FIELD OF THE FINANCIAL SERVICES

The main core of these financial services is the mass of data compiled for each company, kept current through periodic supplements. In several instances, this information includes a brief history of the company and its operations, description of the business and products, a list of principal plants and properties, officers, and directors, the date of the annual meeting, a comparative balance sheet and income account, descriptions of the funded debt and of the capital stock, and the dividend record. In many cases the market price for the capital stock for a period of years is given.

One of the best known of all security services is *Moody's Manual of Investment, American and Foreign.* This service, covering several thousand companies, banks, municipalities, governments, and other business organizations is composed of five annual volumes plus a semiweekly supplement for each. They are: (1) *Banks—Insurance—Real Estate—Investment Trusts;* (2) *Governments;* (3) *Industrials;* (4) *Public Utilities;* (5) *Transportation.*

Besides the information given for each company covered, each volume contains a section which lists data pertinent to that particular industry. For example, *Moody's Banks* lists the 300 largest banks in the United States, and consumer installment credit statistics; *Moody's Industrials* will give a chronological list of maturing industrial bonds; and *Moody's Transportation* (formerly *Moody's Railroads*) will give a definition and list of Class I railways, general financial statistics of Class I railways, and information about the Interstate Commerce Commission.

Possibly the most interesting of these manuals is the one devoted to governments. Here will be found, in addition to the data about government finance, national, state, and municipal, information pertaining to national income, production, and similar items which are vital to the success of any government. Much of this information is included for both the United States and many foreign governments.

Other Moody publications devoted to information about individual companies are *Moody's Dividend Record* and *Moody's Bond Record.* The *Dividend Record* is a semiweekly cumulative record which gives detailed information about dividends. The *Bond Record* is a semimonthly publication giving quotations on approximately 7000 bond issues; detailed statistical information as to earnings, market prices, and amount outstanding is given for approximately 3000 issues. Moody's bond rating is included for most issues.

Another useful security service, differing greatly from Moody's in its format, is Standard & Poor's *Corporation Records.* This six-volume loose-leaf service covers in detail the leading investor-interest corporations. Included in the information given are a brief history of each company and its operations, descriptions of business and products manufactured, list of officers and directors, comparative income and balance sheet data for a period of several years, description of indebtedness and capital stock, and dividend record.

This service is kept current by the issuance of supplements every two months. In addition to the supplements for the six basic volumes, Standard & Poor's issue a *Daily News Section* five times per week (Monday through Friday). The well-indexed *Daily News Section* contains on a more current basis the same type of information found in the basic six volumes.

Other helpful publications of Standard & Poor's are their *Security Owner's Stock Guide,* their *Bond Guide,* and their *Weekly Dividend Record.* In the *Security Owner's Stock Guide* will be found brief company and industry data, including type of business, market or markets on which the stock is listed, price range, brief dividend record, and financial position of each company. This manual is published monthly. The *Bond Guide,* published semimonthly, supplies essential information for the bond investor, including call price, interest dates, and bond quotations. The *Weekly Dividend Record* contains full details on dividend announcements, rights, stock redemptions, and other factors concerning dividends. Each weekly issue is cumulative, and the monthly cumulative section covers the year to date. This publication also gives ex-dividend plans of the major stock exchanges.

The *Fitch Service* is another leading investment service appearing in various sections. Noteworthy among these are *Daily Dividend and Redemptions, News Earnings and Descriptions* (weekly) *Monthly Stock Record, Weekly Bond Record,* and the *Fitch Survey,* a weekly review and forecast of markets and business considering industries as a whole as well as individual corporations.

ADVISORY AND FORECASTING SERVICES

In addition to the security services, the would-be investor should become familiar with the advisory and forecasting services. Rather than emphasizing specific company data, the advisory and forecasting services give information on the trend of the stock market, a description, analysis, and outlook for specific industries, and stock and bond quotations. Included with the charts, graphs, statistical tables, and other factual data are general comments on the future picture of the industry and company under consideration.

Along with their excellent security service, an advisory service, *Trade and Securities,* is issued by Standard & Poor's. Its sections include the *Industry Surveys, Statistics,* and the *Outlook. Industry Surveys* is primarily designed to indicate how the various industries and their respective companies are performing. Divided into two parts, basic and current, the service presents tables, charts, and indices of various types, while the text carries discussions of such topics as competition, the labor situation, and potential sales, thus giving the investor a bird's-eye view of the factors necessary to investigate before making an investment. The *Outlook* is a weekly stock market letter covering the investment outlook for a wide range and variety of securities. Its aim is to "analyze and project business and market trends." While the publication is primarily designed to give the investor a general picture of the investment field, it contains also articles indicating certain features of the economy that may affect the securities market. *Trade and Securities Statistics,* on the other hand, is a service containing all kinds of business statistics: finance, security prices, commodity prices, cost of living indexes, and others.

In addition to the famous security manuals, Moody's publishes two important services of the advisory type. These are the *Stock Survey* and the *Bond Survey.* Both are weekly and contain cumulative indexes. They are particularly useful for following the trend of the stock and bond markets. Besides containing the usual Moody ratings, market prices, recommendations for purchase, and a general discussion of indivdual stocks and bonds, each issue has an analytic article covering some phase of the economic situation.

Another partially supervisory service of special interest to the chart-minded investor is the weekly loose-leaf *Investographs.* The complete service covers 250 stocks and 22 major industries. Included in the service are company reports and such charts as *Investograph Comparative Market Charts, Corporate Investographs, Industry Composites, General Business,* etc. The *Weekly Investment Letter* appraises the market situation, business conditions, groups of industries, and specific companies, and forecasts future developments.

All in all, there are many publications devoted to the security market, both duplicating each other and providing special interpretation. For example, *Investment Companies,* published by Arthur Wiesenberger & Company, is a valuable compendium of information on investment companies and mutual funds, explaining their functions and uses to the investor. It includes data on the background, management policy, and other salient features of all leading companies, together with management results, income records, dividend records, price ranges, and comparative operations.

Data on thousands of unlisted and inactive stocks are found in the *National Daily Quotation Service,* a wire service quoting security offerings and wants of leading investment houses.

Still another specialized tool is the *Fisher Manual of Valuable and Worthless Securities.* This is most valuable in tracing active, little-known, dormant, and inactive corporations, as well as those that have merged, reorganized, liquidated, dissolved, or lost their charters. As one feature it shows the years in which securities became worthless.

INCOME TAX AND OTHER LOOSE-LEAF SERVICES

The advent of the federal income tax laws brought intensive development of the loose-leaf services, since in this field change is continuous, and current information is imperative. Income tax and other regulatory services are designed so that continuous revisions can be accomplished within the basic volume or volumes. Such changes consist of revisions in the basic material, addition of new material on rulings and decisions, as well as complete editorial analysis of these developments. With the loose-leaf form of service the user has available current information in one place. Each service is devoted to one special topic, or a group of closely related topics, such as federal income taxes, labor laws, or other topics in which constant revision is necessary.

Although all such services are similar in arrangement, the publishers include complete information on how best to use each one. A typical service is arranged to include: (1) the text of the statute; (2) the basic text or compilation, based on the law, regulations, and decisions; (3) a section on forms; (4) the current matter section; (5) a cross-reference table or index for locating current developments; and (6) the index. To use these services effectively the index or indexes must be consulted. There may be one master index for the entire service and/or each section may have its own detailed index.

Perhaps the most important of these services for their general use are those on federal income tax regulations, of which the Commerce Clearing House *Standard Federal Tax Service* and the Prentice-Hall *Federal Tax Service* are outstanding examples. Both publishers offer their federal tax service in a one-volume and a multivolume edition. For most businessmen the one-volume edition will be adequate, since it contains the federal tax laws in a simplified form. For the tax accountant or lawyer and others who have need for a detailed description of the tax laws, the multivolume edition is necessary. This covers in great detail the laws, decisions, opinions, forms, and all the other myriad details that are of prime importance.

With the growth and increasing regulation of business firms in the United States, business management has found a knowledge of business and corporate regulations essential. To aid in solution of such problems, Prentice-Hall started their *Corporation Service*. This two-volume work is designed to furnish a convenient means for ascertaining the current law, practice, and procedure of corporations. It includes national laws and regulations, the laws of the forty-eight states, the District of Columbia, and Hawaii, and so provides information about the number of incorporators required in any state, the requirements for interstate business, and the rights and liabilities of stockholders, directors, and officers.

SOURCES OF INFORMATION ON SERVICES

Since the expanding interests of business and the recognized value of pooled information and its interpretations by trained observers have led to the vigorous growth of such information agencies, some guide to the multitude of existing services, their coverage, and frequency was a logical outcome. The *Handbook of Commercial and Financial and Information Services* published by the Special Libraries Association contains descriptions of 577 current services. Together with the information on the needs met by the various services, it includes the publication address and the cost. Discussions of service collections, their use, and extent are included in *Business and the Public Library* and *Public Library Service to Business.*

Services planned for one function frequently have a limited market, with the result that information on the existence of a special type is not always easily procured. Public libraries such as Newark, Cleveland, Chicago, and Boston, where specialized service to business has been developed over many years, are among the best sources of information. As the main storehouses for accumulated business data, they are frequently approached by publishers in connection with new enterprises, and thus they either have in their collections or have knowledge of the existence and subject matter of many services. A visit or a letter to any one of these large business departments in public libraries may result in procurement of the desired information whether at first hand or as a result of investigation. Since such information can be useful not only to the inquirer, but for the library's own files, an investigation of this sort is a natural and logical step. The answers may usually be secured through the many information contacts maintained by these specialists in business information.

A second valuable source of information about the possible existence of a service is the Special Libraries Association. While the business resources in a public library such as Cleveland or Newark will include many services and the staff will know of many more, the information experts of the large advertising agencies, the insurance companies, the financial institutions, and the industrial or service institutions each may have additional knowledge of publications serving their fields. An inquiry addressed to the Association may result in the required information. All libraries are linked in the common effort to supply information. The approach to it may be made through the public, special, or college library door, whichever is most easily accessible.

chapter IX

Books and Other Media in Their Business Function

Development of business books. Agencies in the promotion of business literature. Research organizations and their work. Books and their use. Guides to book evaluation. Maps and atlases for business use. Films as information sources. Business history.

DEVELOPMENT OF BUSINESS BOOKS

While services, pamphlets, and magazines rank high as sources of business information, books still take first place for detailed comprehensive analysis of phases of business development or for serious study of economic forces. The expanding interest in analytical studies is indicated by the changes and intensive treatment of many subjects hitherto neglected.

The last thirty years have witnessed a great increase in business book publication, with several shifts in major interest. In the decade 1910-20, books on efficiency, both personal and industrial, were in demand. The activities of the efficiency experts had focused attention on this function of management, and works by Gilbreth, Taylor, and Gantt stimulated other texts along these lines. In the booming twenties, however, another type of literature was sought. The stock market fever was at its height, and books on investment and discussion of equities crowded the presses. A reflection of this demand for speculative expansion rather than sound groundwork appeared in the many texts on sales campaigns.

But the 1930's brought a sadder and wiser day, and the reaction from overexpansion was a swing to a concept of careful cost analysis, new statistical interpretations, market research based on factual studies, and a realization that depleted consumer incomes meant closer investigation of production costs and of competitors' offerings. Again, public opinion brought about the inevitable development of closer relations between government and business, and this in turn stimulated texts on the problem. The expanding program of social legislation required authoritative consideration of necessary techniques that would adjust the interrelations of the government and business. Accounting methods, industrial relations, advertising programs, corporation policies, all required re-examination in the light of these changing conditions. Against such needs a publication program adequately searching the new horizons was developed.

Until 1930, business executives were content, in most cases, to leave to "professors" the study of economic forces. But the pressing need for a better understanding of why certain untoward developments had taken place led to a growing interest in books approaching current problems from the economic standpoint. No longer could business follow a policy of "the public be damned." A public relations program that could develop mutual understanding and cooperation became a first necessity. The urgency of better public relations was matched by the necessity for constructive labor relations. Intensive demand for thoughtful analysis and a constructive approach to business policies laid a new stress on the desirability of reorientation of the business book publication program.

AGENCIES IN THE PROMOTION OF BUSINESS LITERATURE

The development of collegiate and graduate schools of business has deepened the interest in business research. Their students have been required to investigate the literature and supplementary statistical data bearing on particular problems. Studies that are part of graduate work in business administration have led to an increase in authoritative and analytical treatment of business affairs. A major contribution of this type is the series of *Harvard Business Studies,* based on the case method and including exhaustive statistical studies and records such as Hower's *History of an Advertising Agency at Work,* Baxter's *House of Hancock,* and Moore's *Timing a Century.*

Important sources of current business information which have considerable prestige are the bureaus of business research operated by the many leading colleges and universities with a curriculum of concentrated study in business and economics. With the growing tendency to preface a business career with an education in business administration and economics almost as exacting as the requirements for the professions, enrollment in such courses has greatly increased in the past quarter century.

As the teaching corps has expanded, there has been an extension of research activities and an increase in the number of publications in this field, carrying the prestige of university sponsorship. Frequently, documented by top experts and containing original research, such works are often considered authoritative. Universities with extensive graduate programs in business administration and economic theory may issue books, pamphlets, and leaflets with material that cannot be obtained elsewhere.

Some of the material may be primarily of local interest, such as Boston University's *New England Community Statistical Abstracts*. Some may express opinions and discuss theories affecting the whole social structure, like the books on public opinion and propaganda, published by Princeton University Press.

Many universities regularly issue periodicals on business such as the *Harvard Business Review* and the *Journal of Marketing* published by the School of Retailing, New York University. Masters' and doctors' theses are usually available by interlibrary loan from the institutions which conferred the degrees.

RESEARCH ORGANIZATIONS AND THEIR WORK

Along with the educational institutions, the research organizations have done much to provide a solid foundation of scientific analysis and historical interpretation. The National Bureau of Economic Research, for example, in its work on estimates of national income, had laid the statistical groundwork used in the reports by the Bureau of Foreign and Domestic Commerce initiated in 1933. *The National Income and Its Composition* and *The Output of Manufacturing Industries, 1899-1937* by the National Bureau of Economic Research are two outstanding examples of such statistical studies. Other contributions in this field as well as exhaustive work in cost of living, wage movements, and other economic problems have appeared under the imprint of the National Industrial Conference Board, a leading organization in the cooperative study of economics by economists and businessmen since its founding in 1916.

Of the foundations established for economic research, the Twentieth Century Fund and the Brookings Institution have made extensive studies for publication and wide distribution. The Twentieth Century Fund was founded to search out underlying economic influences, the knowledge of which would be useful in the solution of serious current problems. *Financing the Consumer* by Evans Clark grew out of the Fund's interest in the American credit union movement. Later work has been focused on the need for rebuilding a sound and prosperous system following the war. In the study *America's Needs and Resources* by Dr. J. Frederic Dewhurst, the Fund has presented a comprehensive analysis of America's human and industrial capacity and resources.

One of the primary purposes in the organization of the Brookings Institution, in addition to its interest in the general field of economics, was to enable it to serve as an aid in development of sound national policies based on scientific research in the social sciences. These studies have been made generally available through publication and are illustrated by *Income and Economic Progress* on the distribution of wealth and income and its effect on the country's growth.

Another more recent organization, the Committee for Economic Development has also utilized organized thought in attacking economic problems through employment of noted economists and experts in the business field. Here, too, a rewarding series of publications has resulted. Its support of investigations of basic problems by economists, supplemented by discussion with industrial leaders and scholastic authorities, is an interesting trend of the times. Publication follows both the economists' study and a related policy statement by the CED trustees. Each study benefits from the long series of discussions, but the final publications, not only of the trustees but of the investigator, are each unrestricted by the conclusions of the other.

Businessmen today recognize that many problems arise which can be solved only by extensive research, based on information culled from many sources by experts who have had both long familiarity with such sources and professional training in the techniques of research. Such research may be done by the special research department of a large company. In other cases, members of trade associations may use their research facilities in the preparation of data. Too, in many instances, advertising agencies do research for their clients.

When such service is not available, independent research agencies may be employed on a fee basis. Marketing research agencies may make studies of customer buying habits through interviews and questionnaires, survey the use of dwellings and business properties, do comparison shopping, establish radio-program ratings, and organize food demonstrations.

Obviously, it is impossible to compile a complete list of such commercial organizations doing business research, but a helpful guide to anyone considering marketing research projects is Bradford's *Marketing Research Agencies in the United States and the World.* This directory has an alphabetical finding list by name, a geographical grouping, and a classified list according to the type of research. This list is of particular value, since certain agencies limit their research to such specialized activities as making marketing maps, conducting public opinion polls, compiling statistics, and testing products.

Besides the brief description of each agency mentioned, this book includes its address, type of work, names of officers, date of founding, and number on staff. An additional feature is a list of independent marketing and research agencies in foreign countries, including the forty-two foreign credit offices of Dun and Bradstreet and affiliates of International Gallup polls. Dr. Bradford suggests that the prospective client first formulate his problem, find out what agencies specialize in such research, then by inquiry and correspondence, determine which concern is likely to do the work in satisfactory fashion.

Another list of such research agencies is *Market Research Sources,* which lists 234 commercial organizations doing marketing research. However, this list contains names of private concerns whose research departments function primarily for their employees.

Extensive research in the field of production may entail employment of the services of a management consultant or industrial engineer. Introduction of pension plans, complications in accounting due to increased taxation, time and motion studies, job evaluation, efforts of the intelligent business leader to appraise budget performance, plant layout and modernization, wage incentives, and new methods of inventory control are making it increasingly necessary to seek expert help from outside consultants. The Association of Consulting Management Engineers, Inc., New York, has published a *Directory of Memberships and Services,* which lists the members and describes their experiences and services.

The growth and importance of industrial scientific research has been one manifestation of this scientific era, and the future may see an even closer relationship between industrial research and business. An acknowledgment of this relationship by the National Research Council, National Academy of Science, Washington, D.C., is their publication, *Industrial Research Laboratories in the United States.* This book lists laboratories doing industrial development work, with a description of their staff and principal activities, and indicates those providing consultation service. It has also a subject index to its research programs. An appendix lists laboratories of universities and colleges offering research services to industry, and certain laboratories maintained by the federal government which provide scientific advice upon request.

BOOKS AND THEIR USE

Among the trade press, Prentice-Hall, Harper, Ronald, Wiley, and McGraw-Hill have done much to raise the standards of business books and to fulfill the growing requirements of sound factual treatments of business problems. Other agencies that have helped to extend the boundaries of business knowledge are the Special Libraries Association and the Newark Public Library. Both in its conferences and through articles in *Special Libraries,* that Association has focused attention on needed publications and the uses of available business literature. Its department "Business Book Review Digest," published from February 1930 to April 1935 in *Special Libraries,* made available evaluation of current publications. The Newark Public Library, through the staff of the Business Library, was the first organization to provide a comprehensive bibliography of business books in its *1600 Business Books, 2400 Business Books,* and *Business Books 1920-1926* published in 1916, 1920, and 1926, respectively.

The specific use to which business books are put is indicated by the records of such a collection as that of the Newark Business Library. Some years ago, an analysis of the books borrowed showed the subjects most popular with business readers were accountancy, investment, real estate, salesmanship, advertising, marketing, banking, insurance, and business English. Of these subjects the one that brought the greatest demand for books was accountancy. This interest may be laid to the many detailed uses and treatments of accounting principles. Where a general discussion of advertising, sales management, personnel relations, factory organization may be useful to the majority of readers in these subjects, accountants need particularized material, such as methods for accounting in a mail-order business, in cooperative stores, administration of an estate, accounting for the executive, for branch houses, for associations, and many other detailed situations. Accounting, like other business tools, constantly extends its usefulness and new methods of treating costs, of presentation of cost figures for public understanding or ways to simplify the balance sheet, etc., have resulted in many challenging publications.

In recent years there has been a marked increase in the reading of general business texts. A widespread conviction has developed that current and authentic information is necessary not only in evaluating an industry or for weighing investment trends. One value of up-to-date and sound information lies in the part such knowledge plays in equipping the individual to meet opportunities. The increasing number of standard business texts with their continuing improvement in preparation and quality serve this purpose. The beginner in industry, the man of ten or fifteen years experience, the executive of long standing, all find material for their special needs. To deal with the flood of information pouring from the press, some method of selection must be followed. Here the standard question of how authentic, how biased, and how current is the data must not be forgotten.

GUIDES TO BOOK EVALUATION

Important sources of current listings for books are the weekly bulletins of Public Affairs Information Service, the book review section of the *New York Sunday Times,* and other publications. Book lists covering either special subjects or current books appear in *Business Information Sources,* issued at irregular intervals by the Business Information Bureau of the Cleveland Public Library, and *Business Literature,* the monthly bulletin of the Business Library of the Newark Public Library. This last bulletin, issued ten times a year since 1928, reflects changing business conditions, and in its cumulated volumes provides a record of the business texts that have proved of particular value in that period. The issues for April and May, 1950 contain a comprehensive list of periodicals regularly reviewing such volumes. Some business books are mentioned in the *Technical Book Review Index.* As a guide to additional information, *Business and the Public Library* is useful for its inclusion of a list of magazines publishing business book announcements and reviews, calling special attention to those with long reviews.

From time to time extensive annotated booklists on special subjects have been prepared by university bureaus, by trade associations, or by public libraries. An excellent illustration of one such publication is the *Office Library of an Industrial Relations Executive,* a publication of the Industrial Relations Section of Princeton University. Another, *Books for the Advertising Man,* through the original list and its supplements, covers books in this category since 1923 and represents a major contribution to the business executive on the part of the Advertising Federation of America. The *Business Bookshelf* published by the Newark Public Library represents its answer at one period to the frequent question, "What business books should we buy?"

MAPS AND ATLASES FOR BUSINESS USE

Any businessman concerned with marketing a product, with exporting and importing, with transportation, with pipe lines, or with any of a myriad of problems may want at his elbow at least one good atlas such as the *Encyclopedia Britannica World Atlas.* This contains physical and political maps, geographical comparisons, a glossary of geographical terms, a gazetteer index, a geographical summary, and world spheres of influence. Another of the same quality is *Hammond's New World Atlas* which contains new historical, economic, political, and physical maps of the world in color with complete indexes. The businessman interested in marketing, however, might well consider either adding to the above or substituting Rand McNally's *Commercial Atlas and Marketing Guide,* since it includes marketing maps as well.

Invaluable too for the sales manager and sales force of a company are such tools as the Hearst Corporation's *State Marketing Maps* and the Department of Commerce's *Economic Development Atlas,* showing recent changes in regions and states. Less recent yet helpful in some lines is the *1941 Atlas of Wholesale Dry Goods Trading Areas.* For those interested in the layout of a city or county by streets there are the excellent folding maps by Hagstrom Company.

There are still other types of maps that are useful to business people. For instance, a lawyer might wish to check the exact site of an accident, and a real estate man or a banker might wish to know the exact location of a property. Valuable for such purposes are the *Polyconic Maps for Counties* published by Hearne Brothers. The list of sources, *Maps for Sales Executives* issued by *Sales Management,* is an excellent guide to such publications.

FILMS AS INFORMATION SOURCES

Films are used for many purposes by different industries. A large aviation company may use a film to advertise its products. A public utility company may use this medium to supplement its annual report at stockholders' or directors' meetings. The telephone company's films show how to make the phone do a good job for business. The life insurance company's agency department may find films useful in training the company's agents in selling methods. The savings bank, either individually or together with others, may show a film promoting the use of thrift.

Today films are produced by commercial firms, trade associations, and individual firms. One of the best sources of information on current developments is *Business Screen Magazine,* which carries a semiannual index of sponsored films and publishes an *Index of Training Films,* listing industrial and technical motion pictures and slide films for loan, rental, or purchase. *Dun's Review and Modern Industry* runs a monthly list of *Films for Management,* and still another periodical containing a monthly list of industrial films is *Factory Management and Maintenance. Educators Guide to Free Films* and the *Educational Film Guide* are other excellent guides to those available. *The Business Film and Its Function,* a bibliography published in 1950, notes the sources of information available at that time.

BUSINESS HISTORY

It was not until 1925 that business history had its start as a specialized field of historical research. The term *business history* was first used in 1925, and it was in that year that the Business Historical Society was organized at Harvard to promote the collection of business records and the study of the history of business. This was followed by the establishment of a business history chair at Harvard's Graduate School of Business in 1927. Some time later the Business History Foundation was organized.

Business history, as so far developed, has in the main been devoted to the history of individual companies. These range from the scholarly *Harvard Studies in Business History* to the brochures or volumes published by many companies to celebrate various anniversaries. The *Guide to Business History* by Henrietta Larson, published by the Harvard University Press, is the basic volume for use in this field, both for its enlightening discussion and for its descriptive listing of some 5000 items on business history or relating to it. An elementary guide to references on business history, including descriptive notes on some major studies and illustrative anniversary publications, is "Business Histories and Anniversary Publications," in the April 1948 issue of *Business Literature.*

The *Harvard Studies in Business History* represent a scholarly attempt to portray the history of various individual companies and industries, and are profitable information sources for those doing research in these particular fields. Illustrative volumes are Banning's *Commercial Broadcasting Pioneers,* Moore's *Timing a Century, a*

History of the Waltham Watch Company, and Hower's *The History of an Advertising Agency, N. W. Ayer and Son at Work.* Besides the special studies issued by the Harvard University Press there are other noteworthy volumes such as Dutton's *Du Pont, One Hundred and Forty Years,* and Burlingame's *Of Making Many Books,* published by Scribner.

A revealing volume from another angle is *The Business Founding Date Directory,* compiled by Etna M. Kelley. This gives the founding dates of some 9000 companies established prior to 1916, over 100 dating back to 1900 and before. It reflects the growth of business and industry throughout the country in its chronological listing as well as providing information about specific companies through its alphabetical list.

Chief among the other sources of business historical information are the *Bulletin of the Business Historical Society;* company publications such as house organs, annual reports, and trade catalogs; trade journals; trade association publications; government publications; historical society pamphlets; historical and other special libraries; biographical collections and materials; periodicals; newspapers; and general reference works.

part II

INFORMATION SOURCES FOR SPECIAL SUBJECTS

A NOTE OF EXPLANATION

The purpose of this section is to provide a bibliography of the various information sources that may be applied to particular topics. No attempt is made, through listing, to establish a criterion, and with the expanding number of such resources, any effort to be at all inclusive would be futile. What these selections comprise are *illustrations* of publications that have proved invaluable in providing the information needed by those who have used the Business Library in its fifty years of service.

A special effort has been made to list bibliographies, statistical compilations, handbooks, directories, periodicals, and services, since sources of information on these publications are not so generally available as are those on general texts. A limited list of books is given for each topic but primarily to illustrate the range of the treatment rather than to present a basic list. With their steadily increasing number, an adequate, up-to-date list to supplement these references must be made by the individual as occasion demands through current bibliographical tools. The general catalog of the public library and its files of *Public Affairs Information Service,* the *Cumulative Book Index,* and the *Book Review Digest* are important aids in this.

In spite of consistent effort to limit the references to current sources of information, scarcity of material on some subjects necessitated the inclusion of publications of the early 1940's. The lack of current bibliographies in several areas was brought to light also through the compilation of this section.

Much information on the various topics may be gathered through the use of the listed publications. When the latest material or an exhaustive collection is needed, the use of the current bulletins and annual volumes of *Public Affairs Information Service* will lead to additional references, not only in books and magazines but also in the publications of associations and municipal, state, and federal governments of the United States and other English-speaking countries. This source is especially valuable for current references. As a guide to books published over a period of years, the volumes of the *Cumulative Book Index* are the major tools.

chapter X

The Framework for Business Development

Business conditions and economic factors. Business history. Business and government. Business associations.

Business Conditions and Economic Factors

Bibliographies

"Business and Economic Systems," in *A Reading List on Business Administration.* Hanover, N. H., Dartmouth College, Amos Tuck School of Business Administration, 1952.

This sixth revision gives a descriptive guide to some forty books and to many magazines dealing with business and society, business and government, and general business conditions.

"Business Cycles," *Business Literature.* Newark, N.J., Public Library, Vol. XIX, No. 8 (April 1947).

Annotated list of books on the nature of the business cycle, its control, and developing theories on the subject.

"Cooperation for Economic Understanding," *Business Literature.* Newark, N.J., Public Library, Vol. XXV, No. 4 (December 1952).

A note on the program for joint consideration and study of economic problems carried on by associations and universities. Supplemented by bibliographical references.

"Economic Education and Industry," *Business Literature.* Newark, N.J., Public Library, Vol. XXIV, No. 9 (May 1952).

Descriptive list of pamphlets and magazine articles on the cooperative program developed by industry and educational agencies to broaden economic understanding.

"What is Ahead for Business?" *Business Literature.* Newark, N.J., Public Library, Vol. XXVI, No. 9 (May 1954).

One of a series of bibliographies of current references to business conditions prepared annually since 1951 as a supplement to the Rutgers University Annual Business Conference.

Annuals, handbooks, special compilations

Cole, Arthur H., *Measures of Business Change.* Chicago, Irwin, 1952.

A descriptive list of 449 index series showing subject, compiler, frequency, period covered, and basis on which the index is developed. Indicates regional and product indexes.

Economic Almanac, National Industrial Conference Board. New York, Crowell. Annual.

Handbook of economic, business, and labor statistics compiled with the aid of material from Washington sources and a by-product of four decades of fact-finding and fact-furnishing effort.

Handbook of Basic Economic Statistics. Washington, Economic Statistics Bur. Monthly.

A compact, up-to-date source of more than 1500 authentic government-compiled basic statistical series covering most aspects of the national economy. Includes a monthly summary of national business conditions and economic highlights.

Handbook of Labor Statistics. Washington, U.S. Bur. of Labor Statistics, 1950. Supplement, 1951.

Invaluable guide to industry, starting in 1926. All the major statistical series compiled by the Bureau are included. Sections include prices, cost of living, earnings, hours, wage rates, etc.

Horton, Byrne J., *Dictionary of Modern Economics.* Washington, Public Affairs Press, 1948.

A selection of terms which most frequently appear in writings on our present economy, or which help to understand the past as it influenced the present, or are used in business and economics. Includes biographies of economists and statements on laws, institutions, agencies, government and private, and court decisions which have affected our economy.

Statistical Abstract of the United States. Washington, U.S. Bur. Census. Annual.

An accumulation of statistics on American activities and development covering a long period of years. Covers populations, vital statistics, immigration, finance, railroads, commerce, etc. Contains a list of government bibliographies. Fully indexed.

Survey of Current Business, Annual Review Number. Washington, Government Printing Office.

An analysis of the previous year's business highlights. Discusses national income and product, production and trade, and foreign transactions.

Woytinsky, W. S. and Woytinsky, E. S., *World Population and Production.* New York, Twentieth Century Fund, 1953.

Monumental work on the collective resources, economic performance, and promise of all the nations of the world. Excellent source references and hundreds of figures and tables.

Periodicals and services

American Economic Review. Evanston, Ill., American Economic Association. Quarterly.

A periodical devoted to scholarly discussions of current economic problems. Lengthy, detailed, and authoritative book reviews.

Board of Trade Journal. London. Weekly.

Official publication of the British Board of Trade. Covers both domestic and foreign trade from the British point of view. Includes statistics of sales, tariff rulings, and official notices.

Business Week. New York. Weekly.

A leading news publication for commerce and industry. Consists largely of concise stories on specific activities but runs frequent comprehensive studies. Regular features include "Business Barometer," "The Washington Outlook," "Business Outlook," "International Outlook," "New Products," etc.

Changing Times. Washington. Monthly.

General business reading, widely diversified in subjects and geared to the range of interest and experience of the average individual. Treats municipal well-being, developments in an industry, personal problems in their relation to economic welfare, and other subjects on a scale that relates them to individual responsibilities.

Conference Board Business Record. New York, National Industrial Conference Board. Monthly.

Authoritative articles on business conditions with special attention to financial aspects. Includes survey of business opinion on current questions. Lists statistics as business indicators and includes forecasts.

Dun's Statistical Review. New York. Monthly.

Composed wholly of statistical tables, it presents the latest data on bank clearances, business failures, price indices, building permit values, and new business incorporations. Includes a group of economy indicators.

Economic Indicators. Washington, U.S. Congress, Joint Committee on the Economic Report. Monthly.

By employing charts and tables, this publication is made valuable for gaining at a glance, economic data ranging from expenditures for new plant and equipment to corporate profits for various years.

Economist. London. Weekly.

Although published primarily for the British businessman, valuable to Americans for its articles on international finance, world politics, and commercial activities in various countries and regions. "American Survey" contains articles on the political and economic situation in this country. Statistics include data on United Kingdom and British Commonwealth production and consumption, foreign trade, and financial statistics. Contains book reviews, London stock prices, annual reports of various corporations, and notes on company activities.

Federal Reserve Bulletin. Washington, Board of Governors of the Federal Reserve System. Monthly.

Contains articles on national and international trade and finance, official Board announcements, and many tables covering national financial, industrial, and commercial statistics. Other tables regularly cover international financial statistics.

Journal of Commerce. New York. Daily except Saturday and Sunday.

An excellent source for current commodity prices. Presents news on commerce, commodities, and manufacturing as well as general business news. Contains daily market quotations, shipping news, and insurance information.

Kiplinger Washington Letter. Washington, Kiplinger Washington Agency.

Weekly comment on developments in Washington through which observation and interpretation by well-informed observers give businessmen the benefit of a fortunate combination of experience, skill, and qualified selection.

Monthly Labor Review. Washington, Government Printing Office. Monthly.

The medium through which the U.S. Department of Labor publishes its regular monthly reports on such subjects as trends in employment and payrolls, hourly and weekly earnings, weekly working hours, collective agreements, industrial accidents, industrial disputes, and other information.

Review of Economics and Statistics. Cambridge, Mass., Harvard University Press. Quarterly.

Primarily devoted to the enlightenment of economic scientists, its articles are mainly the contributions of members of the Department of Economics at Harvard. Subject matter concerned with broad aspects of economic theory and movements, with emphasis on statistical analysis. Book reviews.

The Statist. London. Weekly.

Current trends in finance, industry, foreign trade, international relations, from the English viewpoint. Regular statistical section, prices; investment data.

Survey of Current Business. Washington, Government Printing Office. Monthly.

The major reporting publication for business statistics, including indexes for income payments, industrial production, commodity prices, statistics on construction and real estate, domestic trade, employment conditions and wages, finance, foreign trade, transportation and communication, products by kind, etc. Some reports on the business situation and particular industries are included.

Treasury Bulletin. Washington, Government Printing Office. Monthly.

This official organ of the Treasury Department consists entirely of statistical tables and charts on all phases of public finance.

Wall Street Journal. New York. Daily except Saturday and Sunday.

A reporter of current doings in financial circles, it carries news that reflects the ways of our economy. Stock market quotations, Dow-Jones averages, and corporation reports are daily features.

General texts

Allen, Frederick Lewis, *The Big Change: America Transforms Itself, 1900-1950.* New York, Harper, 1952.

Fascinating account of how the American standard of living and way of thinking have been changed by a vast expansion of industrial and business activity, accompanied by a multitude of economic, social, and political forces.

Bratt, E. C., *Business Cycles and Forecasting.* Chicago, Irwin, 1948.

Shows the causes of economic change, the techniques for measuring them, and the methods available for forecasting changes.

Burns, Arthur F. and Mitchell, Wesley C., *Measuring Business Cycles.* New York, National Bureau of Economic Research, 1946.

Expands on Mitchell's *Business Cycles: The Problem and Its Setting* and introduces improved measuring techniques. "A Reader's Guide" in the preface shows for which groups each chapter will be of interest.

Bursk, E. C., ed., *Thinking Ahead for Business.* Cambridge, Mass., Harvard University Press, 1952.

Based on the proceedings of the Twenty-First National Business Conference sponsored by the Harvard Business School Association in June, 1951. The topics covered are written by outstanding authorities. Valuable selected bibliography included.

Davenport, Russell W. and others, *U.S.A., the Permanent Revolution.* New York, Prentice-Hall, 1951.

A review of fundamental American economic and political principles, their development over the years, and their great importance to an understanding of today's problems.

Dewey, E. R. and Dakin, E. F., *Cycles: The Science of Prediction.* New York, Holt, 1950.

Presents the theory that economic rhythms are regular and predictable, and indicate probabilities ahead in business.

Dewhurst, Frederick and Associates, *America's Needs and Resources.* New York, Twentieth Century Fund, 1955.

Gives an estimate of the country's industrial resources balanced against its probable needs. "A fact book of the American economic system," and "an informed guide for the future." The text is emphasized by numerous charts and tables.

Gambs, J. C., *Man, Money, and Goods.* New York, Columbia University Press, 1952.

Money, banking, business cycles, prices, taxes, and international trade explained in clear nontechnical language. Its lucid and lively style will help the reader to grasp contemporary problems, rising prices, taxes, etc.

Gordon, Robert A., *Business Fluctuations.* New York, Harper, 1952.

Comprehensive authoritative discussion of the problems raised by business fluctuations and the efforts to forecast and control business cycles.

Hansen, Alvin H., *Business Cycles and National Income.* New York, Norton, 1951.

Deals with the nature of business cycles, the theory of income and employment, business-cycle theory, and public policy with regard to business cycles. Includes a comprehensive bibliography.

Keezer, Dexter M., ed., *Making Capitalism Work.* New York, McGraw-Hill, 1950.

A comprehensive analysis of the nation's economy and indication of the steps the authors believe are needed to give capitalism a prosperous future.

Kuznets, Simon, *National Income and its Composition, 1919-1938,* 2 vols. New York, National Bureau of Economic Research, 1941.

The main object of this important study was to arrive at annual estimates of national income since World War I. The broad discussion of the issues makes this work of value to consumers and producers alike. Half of the book is devoted to methodology and data.

Moulton, H. G., *Income and Economic Progress.* Washington, Brookings, 1935.

The last of a series of four studies widely discussed, presenting the results of an investigation of the distribution of wealth and income in relation to economic progress. The preceding studies were: *America's Capacity to Produce, America's Capacity to Consume,* and *Formation of Capital.*

Paton, William A., *Shirtsleeve Economics.* New York, Appleton, 1952.

An informal, easily understood presentation of the fundamentals of economics from a free-enterprise point of view.

Ruggles, Richard, *Introduction to National Income and Income Analysis.* New York, McGraw-Hill, 1949.

After building up national income concepts from the basic accounts of individual homes, firms, and government units, the author leads into a discussion of income analysis. The book closes with two chapters on stability, full employment, and economic policy.

Slichter, Sumner H., *What's Ahead for American Business.* Boston, Little, Brown, 1951.

Points out the changes in institutions and practices, economic conditions, and ideas over the last few decades, and with these as guides, attempts to forecast probable trends in the economy for the foreseeable future.

Woytinsky, W. S. and Associates, *Employment and Wages in the United States.* New York, Twentieth Century Fund, 1953.

Comprehensive survey of the entire labor picture. Contains almost 200 pages of statistical tables.

Business History

Bibliographies

"Business Histories and Anniversary Publications," *Business Literature,* Newark, N.J., Public Library, Vol. XX, No. 8 (April 1948).

A descriptive list of references on the why and how of business histories, and of major illustrations, including anniversary publications for quarter, half, and century old organizations.

Larson, H. M., *Guide to Business History.* Cambridge, Mass., Harvard University Press, 1948.

A comprehensive annotated listing of publications ranging from directories, periodicals, and bibliographies to histories which have a direct or an indirect bearing on business history. The systematic arrangement emphasizes the essential ideas developing within the field.

Annuals, handbooks, special compilations

Historical Statistics of the United States, 1789-1945; A Supplement to the Statistical Abstract. Washington, U.S. Bur. Census, 1949.

Historical statistics that portray the status of the United States in various fields at various times. Compilation of special value because of the otherwise limited accessibility of data.

Periodicals

Business History Review. Boston, Harvard Graduate School of Business Administration. Quarterly.

Relation of business attitudes and actions to social change. Growth of business functions, histories of important firms, and biographies of leading businessmen are all included.

Directories

Kelley, Etna M., *Business Founding Date Directory.* Scarsdale, N.Y., Morgan & Morgan, 1954.

A chronological and alphabetical listing of some 9000 American companies established before 1916 with brief descriptive note on companies listed.

General texts

Banning, W. P., *Commercial Broadcasting Pioneers. The WEAF Experiment 1922-1926.* Cambridge, Mass., Harvard University Press, 1946.

Bridges an important historical gap in the early history of the broadcasting industry. The pioneering steps and decisions are detailed in chronological sequence.

Baxter, W. T., *House of Hancock; Business in Boston, 1724-1775.* Cambridge, Mass., Harvard University Press, 1945.

The historian's craftmanship at its best, with many original documents incorporated at length and footnotes providing authentic documentations.

This excellent picture of the colonial business period makes the House of Hancock an illuminating contribution in the field of business history.

Burlingame, Roger, *Of Making Many Books, a Hundred Years of Reading, Writing, and Publishing*. New York, Scribner, 1946.

Feverish and not so feverish exploits and decisions in the never-placid publishing trade as exemplified by the House of Scribner. Conservative trade ways are interwoven with delightful anecdotes.

Dutton, W. S., *DuPont—One Hundred and Forty Years*. New York, Scribner, 1949.

The biography of a great business that has moved from explosives to pervasive chemical developments, reflecting the changing industrial life of the nation.

Gras, N. S. B., *Business and Capitalism; an Introduction to Business History*. New York, Crofts, 1939.

Fascinating well-illustrated book on the evolution of capitalism from the earliest times down to the present. Bibliography and a long list of suggested studies are included.

Hower, R. M., *The History of an Advertising Agency—N. W. Ayer and Son at Work 1869-1949*. Cambridge, Mass., Harvard University Press, 1949.

Includes a general history of the agency, giving the growth of the service and an analysis of particular aspects, including policies in dealing with advertisers and relations with other agencies.

James, Marquis and James, B. R., *Biography of a Bank*. New York, Harper, 1954.

The story of the Bank of America, the world's largest bank and the colorful career of its founder told by a Pulitzer prize winner.

Miller, William, ed., *Men in Business; Essays in the History of Entrepreneurship*. Cambridge, Mass., Harvard University Press, 1952.

The development of business in the Western world in the nineteenth and twentieth centuries, as shown through the correspondence of businessmen of those times. Written by twelve economists and historians.

Moore, C. W., *Timing a Century; History of the Waltham Watch Company.* Cambridge, Mass., Harvard University Press, 1945.

The intricacies of the vicissitudes of the company's career under strongly differing leadership and with widely ranging conditions of prosperity and the reverse are described in engaging style with pertinent illustrations.

Walker, James Blaine, *Epic of American Industry.* New York, Harper, 1949.

Interesting informal account of important industrial events over the past 300 years. Bibliography included.

Business and Government

Bibliographies

"Business Observers for Federal Activities," *Business Literature.* Newark, N.J., Public Library, Vol. XIX, No. 5 (January 1947).

Descriptive list of services and magazines reporting government developments.

"Priorities in Government Tools for the Business Man," *Business Literature.* Newark, N.J., Public Library, Vol. XXIII, No. 2-4 (October-December 1950).

Three issues featuring the most basic government publications. Sources of information and guides to use are listed, as well as statistical compilations, directories, periodicals, marketing aids, foreign trade tools, and various important series.

"Put Your Business House in Order," *Business Literature.* Newark, N.J., Public Library, Vol. XIX, No. 9 (May 1947).

Annotated list of government publications of aid to the small businessman.

State Manual Procurement Guide (Hotaling, D. O.), New York, *Special Libraries* (August 1953).

Lists available state manuals together with frequency and price. Contains advice on how to obtain them.

"Taxes and Management," *Business Literature*. Newark, N.J., Public Library, Vol. XXIV, No. 4 (December 1951).

Annotated bibliography on taxation and its effect on corporation development.

"Your Vote and the Economic Climate," *Business Literature*. Newark, N.J., Public Library, Vol. XXV, No. 3 (November 1952).

Annotated bibliography of magazine articles bearing on the relation of governmental change to economic problems such as cost of living, taxation, governmental controls.

Annuals, handbooks, special compilations

Book of the States, 1954-1955. Chicago, Council of State Governments, 1954. Supplements.

Authoritative source of information on financing and functional activities of state governments. Includes listings of officials, etc.

Facts and Figures on Government Finance. New York, Tax Foundation. Annual.

Presents information on the fiscal activities of federal, state, and local governments. Charts and tables cover the economy, business, government expenditures, taxations, revenues, debt, and social insurance and related programs.

Municipal Year Book. Chicago, International City Managers Association. Annual.

Data on American cities include population and economic status; personnel and pay rates; municipal activities; directories of officials and statistical charts.

Statesman's Yearbook. New York, Macmillan. Annual.

A concise, reliable manual of descriptive and statistical information about world governments. Includes data on form of government, area, population, education, economic and social conditions, with bibliography.

United States Government Organization Manual. Washington, Federal Register Division. Annual.

Describes the organization and function of every agency of the government in the legislative, executive, and judicial branches. Includes charts showing the administrative organization of each branch, major department, etc.

Periodicals and services

Congressional Quarterly. Washington. Quarterly.

A service that gives background on congressional activity and lobbying angles, record of votes, committee action, bills introduced, press opinions, pressure-group activities. A well-arranged factual service planned for editors and commentators and useful for study of data and action in relation to specific bills.

Federal Register. Washington, National Archives and Records Service. Daily except Sunday, Monday, and day following an official federal holiday.

Includes presidential proclamations, executive orders, documents or classes of documents having general applicability and legal effects, agency organization, procedures and regulations, and notices of proposal rules making. Indexes are published monthly, quarterly, and annually.

Federal Tax Guide. Chicago, Commerce Clearing House.

Consists of an annual "Guide" volume and a "Supplemental" volume. Emphasis placed on federal income tax, but essential details about the estate, gift, and miscellaneous taxes are included. The "Guide" contains explanations, income tax regulations, and selected precedent-creating authorities. The "Supplemental" volume carries texts of the law and additional regulations. The comprehensive *Standard Federal Tax Reporter*, published by the same organization with weekly revisions, supplies the text of statutes, regulations, and decisions with full information and interpretation.

Federal Tax Services. New York, Prentice-Hall.

This six-volume service contains complete reprints of the laws, with regulations, rulings, and decisions, as well as editorial explanations.

Kiplinger Washington Letter. Washington, Kiplinger Washington Agency.

Weekly comment on developments in Washington through which observation and interpretation by well-informed observers give businessmen the benefit of a fortunate combination of experience, skill, and qualified selection.

Synopsis of United States Government Proposed Procurement Sales and Contract Awards. Washington, U.S. Dept. Commerce. Daily (Monday-Friday).

Proposed procurement by department and agency with information on quantity, invitation number, or proposed and opening date, and contract awards by department or agency and information on quantity, dollar value, and contractor's name and address. Includes proposed procurements to be awarded to small firms.

Taxes, the Tax Magazine. Chicago, Commerce Clearing House. Monthly.

Washington tax talk. Interpretations, articles of special interest in tax field; book reviews; Canadian tax field.

United States Government Advertiser. Washington, U.S. Government Advertiser, Inc. Daily.

Contains U.S. Government procurement and award lists. News items on government activities and other miscellaneous data.

Directories

Congressional Directory. Washington, Government Printing Office. Annual.

Includes biographical list of members of Congress, members of committees, personnel of government departments, foreign diplomatic and consular representatives and personnel of United States foreign service, press representatives, and much other related information.

Public Administration Organization. Chicago, Public Administration Clearing House, 1954.

A directory and descriptive listing on membership, finances, staff activities, affiliations, and publications of unofficial organizations in the field of public administration, including many trade associations.

General texts

Blachly, Frederick F. and Oatman, Miriam E., *Federal Regulatory Action and Control.* Washington, Brookings, 1940.

A scholarly presentation of the organization, legal status, and relationships of the federal administrative system.

Butters, J. K., *Effects of Taxation: Corporate Mergers.* Boston, Harvard Business School, 1951.

Analyzes the nature of the tax motivations for the sale of closely held companies and the circumstances under which they are likely to exert strong pressure on the owners.

Hall, C. A., Jr., *Effects of Taxation on Executive Compensation and Retirement Plans.* Boston, Harvard Business School, 1951.

Examines the various forms of executive compensation, describing in detail their advantages and disadvantages from the standpoint of both corporate and individual taxation. Also deals with the effects of various specific forms of compensation and retirement plans, on executives' mobility, performance, and retirement.

Kimmel, L. H., *Taxes and Economic Incentives.* Washington, Brookings, 1950.

Deals primarily with taxpayers' reactions and their repercussions in the economic sphere. The effects of taxes on decisions with respect to investment and economic expansion are a major consideration.

Lyon, Leverett, Abramson, Victor, and Associates, *Government and Economic Life.* Washington, Brookings, 1940.

An analysis of the relationship of government to economic life as a whole in terms of fundamental economic and social functions and fundamental governmental activities.

Mund, Vernon A., *Government and Business.* New York, Harper, 1950.

Considers the role of government in maintaining and regulating the economic system, the background and reasons for government intervention in business, the forms of government intervention, and the policies adopted by government to promote the public interest in the economic field.

Nourse, Edwin G., *Price Making in a Democracy.* Washington, Brookings, 1944.

Shows how the private-enterprise system works from the point of view of price and production policies.

Sanders, T. H., *Effects of Taxation on Executives.* Boston, Harvard Business School, 1951.

Discusses the effect of taxes on executives' efforts, the intensity and duration of their business careers, retirement, and their efforts to attain personal financial competence.

Steiner, George A., *Government's Role in Economic Life.* New York, McGraw-Hill, 1953.

Comprehensive analysis of a subject affecting all areas of our life. The three main divisions of the book are: "I Evolution of the Subject"; "II The Problem in Two Decades of National Crises"; "III The Problem Today and Tomorrow."

Business Associations

Bibliographies

"Trade Associations as Sources of Information," *Business Literature,* Newark, N.J., Public Library, Vol. XVII, No. 10 (June 1945).

A brief discussion of the functions of trade associations together with an annotated list of publications on trade associations in general and illustrative association publications.

Periodicals

American Trade Association Executives Journal. Washington. Quarterly.

General articles on trade association developments, current items on activities, publications, and news of the field of particular interest to the members.

Directories

American Trade Association Executives—Membership Directory. Washington, 1953.

Includes lists of members arranged alphabetically by individual and association as well as geographically and classified by industry.

Foreign Trade Associations in the United States. Washington, U.S. Dept. Commerce, 1945.

Includes basic data on 700 cooperative associations in 140 cities, 400 trade associations, and 200 other organizations; these represent business, labor, agriculture, and the professions.

Market Research Sources, pp. 149-172. Washington, U.S. Dept. Commerce, 1950.

This guide to marketing data lists in one chapter the associations carrying on special work in this field and notes their publications.

National Associations of the United States. Washington, U.S. Dept. Commerce, 1949.

A directory containing information on 4000 trade, professional, civic, and other associations. Includes data on size of staff and membership.

General texts

Mitchell, Walter, Jr., *How to Use Your Trade Association.* New York, Prentice-Hall, 1951.

Comprehensive discussion of the place of the trade association and its potentialities, including discussion of specific activities of trade associations today.

Patterson, John C., *Association Management.* New York, Harper, 1952.

Using the experiences of many successful associations as illustrations, the author covers all the most important aspects of association activities. Office management, committees, fund-raising research, and government relations are only a few of the subjects covered.

Trade Association Activities. Washington, U.S. Dept. Commerce, 1927.

While out of date, a good descriptive study of the service of trade associations in the field of scientific and economic research, statistical compilation, standardization of commodities, development of foreign trade, etc.

Trade Association Survey. Temporary National Economic Committee Monograph 18. Washington, Government Printing Office, 1941.

An over-all picture, analyzing characteristics and activities of trade associations. Extensive discussion of statistical services and methods by which information is disseminated. Many tabulations on activities. Includes a list of trade associations classified by industry.

chapter XI

Basic Factors in Business Development

Banking and finance. Investments. Insurance. Real estate and construction. Foreign trade. Public utilities, including transportation.

Banking and Finance

Bibliographies

"Banking Today," *Business Literature.* Newark, N.J., Public Library, Vol. XVIII, No. 4 (December 1945).

An annotated list prepared as a supplement to an American Institute of Banking seminar on current banking problems.

Bibliography for a Bank Library of Less Than 200 Volumes. Madison, Wis., School of Banking, University of Wisconsin, 1951.

A selected list of books, periodicals, and reports on banking and allied subjects prepared through the cooperation of bankers, librarians, and the deans of Schools of Commerce with a committee of the School of Banking faculty.

"Consumer Credit," *Business Literature.* Newark, N.J., Public Library, Vol. XVIII, No. 8 (April 1946).

Annotated list of references to the theory and practice of consumer credit and methods of informing the consumer. Includes a list of the periodicals on the subject.

Cumulative Catalogue of Theses 1937-1951, Graduate School of Banking. New York, American Bankers Association, no date.

Descriptive list, alphabetically arranged, of the theses in specialized fields of banking, business, and economics prepared in partial fulfillment of graduation requirements. Subject index included.

Selected Bibliography of Money, Credit, Banking, and Business Finance, compiled by Ray B. Westerfield. Cambridge, Mass., Bankers Publishing Company, 1940.

An unannotated bibliography listing only books. Consists of an index of subjects, an index of books, an index of authors, and an index of publishers.

Annuals, handbooks, special compilations

Banking and Monetary Statistics. Washington, Board of Governors of the Federal Reserve System, 1943.

Makes available in one place and on a uniform basis statistics on banking, monetary, and other financial developments for, with some exceptions, the period 1914 to December, 1941.

Bogen, Jules I., ed., *Financial Handbook.* New York, Ronald, 1948.

A compact presentation of the many aspects of practical finance contributed by authorities in this field. Includes interest and annuity tables, discounts, etc.

Comptroller of the Currency Report. Washington, Government Printing Office. Annual.

The current report of the national banking system is supplemented by tables showing by state the assets and liabilities of all classes of banks. Lists officials of state banking departments, gives number in each class of active banks, totals of assets and liabilities of active banks, 1940 to date, and related data.

Doris, Lillian, ed., *Business Finance Handbook.* New York, Prentice-Hall, 1953.

Attempts to present and offer practical and authoritative solutions to everyday financial problems.

Encyclopedia of Banking and Finance. Garvin, F. L. and Munn, G. G., compilers. Cambridge, Mass., Bankers Publishing Company, 1949.

An invaluable reference work, covering banking, investment, economic, financial, and related legal terms and subjects. Short bibliographies follow the important topics.

Federal Deposit Insurance Corporation Report. Washington, Government Printing Office. Annual.

Data on the operations of the corporation and related legislation and regulations, supplemented by extensive tables on banking developments, including statistics of banks and deposit insurance.

Periodicals and services

American Banker. New York. Daily except Saturday, Sunday, and holidays.

The only daily banking paper. Contains news stories on all aspects of banking in all parts of the country. Includes daily market news, bank statements, official changes, and legal notices. Noted for its annual compilations of banks, savings and loan associations, and investment trusts in order of size.

Auditgram. Chicago, National Association of Bank Auditors and Comptrollers. Monthly.

The only periodical devoted to the interests of the bank auditor and comptroller. Contains articles on operation and control, taxation, and economic conditions. Occasional book reviews.

Bankers Monthly. Chicago. Monthly.

A reliable magazine known especially for its section on equipment and supplies. Contains full-length articles as well as regular departments covering Washington issues, financial highlights, the farm outlook, and news about banks and bankers.

Banking. New York, American Bankers Association. Monthly.

Covers the field of banking from administration and public relations to record details, as well as discussion of broad economic problems. Many special sections on banking news, legal notes, methods, and ideas published intermittently.

Burroughs Clearing House. Detroit, Burroughs Corporation. Monthly.

Contains interesting articles of interest to bankers. Regular features include "Washington Viewpoint," "Personality Spotlight," "Canadian Banking," "Booklet Counter," and "Court Decisions."

Journal of Finance. Chicago, American Finance Association. Quarterly.

Authoritative articles on business, consumer and public finance, investments, and money and banking. Scholarly book reviews.

Monetary Times. Toronto. Monthly.

Articles on financial conditions in Canada and data on bank clearings, exchange quotations, and prices for Canada.

Mortgage Banker. Chicago, Mortgage Bankers Association of America. Monthly.

Official organ of the Association covering current topics of interest in this field. Includes a good statistical section.

Robert Morris Associates Bulletin. Philadelphia, Robert Morris Associates. Monthly.

Excellent little magazine slanted toward the bank credit man and his problems.

Savings and Loan News. Rockford, Ill., United States Savings and Loan League. Monthly.

Presents timely articles of interest to savings and loan officials, facts and figures on savings and loan associations, business and real estate trends, and related topics.

Trusts and Estates. New York. Monthly.

Contains articles of interest to the trustee, administrator, and executor, and a professional investors' digest which includes the "Henry Ansbacher Long Index of Mutual Funds." Regular departments cover court decisions, wills, federal taxes, book reviews, and personnel changes in the trust field.

Directories

Polk's Bankers Encyclopedia. Detroit, Polk.

A complete bank directory arranged by state and giving officers, resources, liabilities, and principal correspondents. Includes information on state officials and regulations as well as lists of investment dealers, directory of legal reserve life insurance companies, and much related material.

Rand McNally Bankers' Directory; the Bankers Blue Book. Chicago, Rand McNally.

An excellent guide to facts and statistics on individual banks all over the world, and a compendium of useful information on various aspects of the American banking system.

General texts

Bradford, Frederick A., *Money and Banking.* New York, Longmans, 1949.

Valuable as an easy-to-read textbook on the financial system.

Chandler, L. V., *Economics of Money and Banking.* New York, Harper, 1948.

Good introduction to the field. Emphasizes basic principles, functions, and operations of our financial system.

Foster, Major B. and others, *Money and Banking.* New York, Prentice-Hall, 1953.

Excellent text on the fundamentals of money and banking with emphasis on the American system, though including three chapters on foreign systems. Interesting historical background chapters. Bibliography after each chapter.

Pease, Robert H., ed., *Mortgage Banking.* New York, McGraw-Hill, 1953.

The first completely descriptive book about making mortgages and on the mortgage banking industry.

Prochnow, Herbert V., ed., *American Financial Institutions.* New York, Prentice-Hall, 1951.

A study of the entire American financial structure with each topic treated by an authority in the particular field. Among topics included are the Federal Reserve System, urban real estate financing, the commodity exchange, credit rating agencies, and personal finance.

Steiner, William H. and Shapiro, Eli, *Money and Banking; an Introduction to the Financial System.* New York, Holt, 1953.

Good text dealing with the broad subjects of money and credit, commercial banking structure and operation; central banking, monetary theory, international finance relations, monetary policy, and financial institutions. Selected references after each chapter.

"Federal Reserve System; Purposes and Functions," *U.S. Federal Reserve System.* Washington, Board of Governors of Federal Reserve System, 1954.

Official account of our central banking system and how it works.

INVESTMENTS

Bibliographies

"Investment Bibliography," in Robbins, Sidney M., *Managing Securities.* Boston, Houghton Mifflin, 1954.

Books, pamphlets, government publications, newspapers, and magazine articles listed in an extensive and well-arranged bibliography.

Investment Bookshelf, compiled by Walter E. Forster. New York, *Library Journal,* Vol. 78, No. 10 (May 15, 1953).

An annotated list covering books on investments in general as well as for the professional trader.

Annuals, handbooks, special compilations

Fisher, Robert D., *Robert D. Fisher Manual of Valuable and Worthless Securities.* New York, Author. Annual.

The Fisher manuals, successors to those of Marvyn Scudder & Company, are most valuable in tracing active, little-known, dormant, and inactive corporations as well as those that have merged, reorganized, liquidated, dissolved, or lost their charters. Shows the year that securities became worthless.

Investment Companies. New York, Wiesenberger, Arthur & Co. Annual.

Valuable compendium of information on investment companies and mutual funds. Explains their functions and uses to the investor and includes data on the background, management policy, and other salient features of all leading companies—management results, income records, dividend records, price ranges, and comparative operations.

Services

Fitch Service. New York, Fitch.

A leading investment service appearing in various sections. Noteworthy among these are *Daily Dividend and Redemptions, News Earnings and Descriptions* (weekly), *Monthly Stock Record, Weekly Bond Record,* and the *Fitch Survey,* a weekly review and forecast of markets and business, considering industries as a whole as well as individual corporations.

Investographs. Rochester, Investograph Service.

Partially supervisory weekly loose-leaf service for the chart-minded investor. Complete service covers 250 stocks and 22 major industries. Included in the service are company reports and such charts as *Investograph Comparative Market Charts, Corporate Investographs, Industry Composites, General Business,* etc. The *Weekly Investment Letter* appraises the market situation, business conditions, groups of industries, and specific companies, and forecasts future developments.

Moody's Investors Service. New York, Moody.

Service consists of several parts. Among the more important are the five annuals, each with semiweekly supplements. These are: (1) *Governments and Municipals;* (2) *Public Utilities;* (3) *Industrials;* (4) *Transportation —Railroads, Airlines, Shipping;* (5) *Banks, Insurance, Real Estate, Investment Trusts.* Also important is *Moody's Stock Survey,* a weekly publication, giving opinions of security market trends, discussing industries, and recommending individual stocks for sale, purchase, or exchange. *Moody's Bond Survey,* also weekly, gives opinion on the security market, discusses individual companies, and recommends individual bonds for sale, purchase, or exchange.

National Daily Quotation Service. New York, National Quotation Bureau.

A service quoting security offerings and wants of leading investment houses. *National Corporation Bond Summary* provides a six-month cumulation of the same information. *National Stock Summary* resembles the *Bond Summary* but includes data on thousands of unlisted and inactive stocks.

Standard Corporation Records. New York, Standard & Poor's.

Service contains factual data on American and Canadian corporations and their securities. It consists of loose-leaf volumes arranged alphabetically by company, a *Daily News* section covering all current corporation news published through the U.S., a *Dividend Section* published daily or weekly, and *Sinking Fund Sheets.*

Standard & Poor's Earnings and Ratings Bond Guide. New York, Standard & Poor's.

A monthly service containing statistical data on various issues, ratings, yield charts, redemption list, and other valuable information.

Standard & Poor's Security Owner's Stock Guide. New York, Standard & Poor's.

A monthly service containing complete statistical tables of common and preferred stocks, purchase recommendations, business forecasts, and other information important to the investor.

Standard & Poor's Trade and Securities. New York, Standard & Poor's.

An economic and investment service which advises on purchase and sale of securities and commodities. It consists of (1) *The Weekly Outlook for the Security Markets;* (2) *Surveys* of all key industries with their securities; (3) *Industry Surveys, Trends and Projections Monthly;* (4) A *Statistical Section.*

Periodicals

Barron's National Business and Financial Weekly. Boston. Weekly.

This highly respected weekly contains current data on government, business, and specific companies. The statistical section includes bond quotations, over-the-counter market, stock quotations, weekly indexes of production and trade, economic and financial indicators, spot prices (Dow Jones averages of 12 commodities), Dow-Jones averages, etc.

Commercial and Financial Chronicle. New York, Semiweekly.

A veritable financial bible. The Monday issue covers general corporation and investment news, bank clearings, state and city bond offerings, redemption calls and sinking fund notices, dividends declared and payable, foreign exchange rates, statement of Federal Reserve Banks, and stock and bond quotations. Thursday's issue contains general articles and news on finance, mutual finance funds, etc.

Financial World. New York. Weekly.

Discussion of investment market with special attention to developments in specific securities.

U.S. Securities and Exchange Commission Statistical Bulletin. Washington, Government Printing Office. Monthly.

Contains charts and tables on nationwide movement of stocks. Includes also tables showing savings of individuals and total current assets and liabilities of corporations.

Wall Street Journal. New York. Daily except Saturday and Sunday.

A reporter of current doings in financial circles, it carries news that reflects the ways of our economy. Stock market quotations, Dow-Jones averages, and corporation reports are daily features.

Directories

Security Dealers of North America. New York, Seibert. Annual.

Security dealers in the United States and Canada with officers, type of securities handled. Geographic arrangement.

General texts

Badger, Ralph E. and Guthmann, H. G., *Investment; Principles and Practices.* New York, Prentice-Hall, 1951.

An excellent book which discusses investment markets, analysis of securities by types, mathematics and mechanics of investments, taxation, the business cycle, and investment policy and practice.

Graham, Benjamin, *The Intelligent Investor.* New York, Harper, 1954.

An excellent, practical, and readable guide for the individual and nonprofessional investor, stressing principles of security selection.

Graham, B. and Dodd, D. L., *Security Analysis, Principles and Techniques.* New York, McGraw-Hill, 1951.

Careful and penetrating study of the broad problems of investment policy.

Jordan, David F. and Dougall, H. E., *Investments.* New York, Prentice-Hall, 1952.

One of the best books on investments, revised to show the influence of World War II, the shift in the capital and securities markets, the growing influence of regulation, the increased interest in common stocks, and other recent developments.

Pickett, R. R. and Ketchum, M. D., *Investment Principles and Policy.* New York, Harper, 1954.

The problems of the individual investor and the points for consideration in the development of his investment program are given first place. Attention is paid to the effect on security prices of political influences. Government supervision of security exchanges and other pertinent topics are discussed.

Sauvain, Harry C., *Investment Management.* New York, Prentice-Hall, 1953.

Develops a method of analysis applicable to investors generally and applies it first to individual investors and then to the various types of investing institutions. Brief bibliography.

Weissman, Rudolph L., *Investment Company and the Investor.* New York, Harper, 1951.

A popularly written book dealing with the operations and policies of investment companies. An excellent guide for the layman.

Insurance

Bibliographies

Creation and Development of an Insurance Library. New York, Special Libraries Association, 1949.

Includes a comprehensive current bibliography for all fields of insurance.

Insurance Book Reviews. Special Libraries Association Insurance Group. Newark, N. J., Mutual Benefit Life Insurance Company.

A briefly annotated list of current publications in all fields of insurance, issued ten times a year.

"Insurance, Miscellaneous Types," *Business Literature.* Newark, N. J., Public Library, Vol. XVIII, No. 10 (June 1946).

Annotated list of references on fire, casualty, liability, and other forms of insurance.

"Life Insurance," *Business Literature.* Newark, N. J., Public Library, Vol. XVIII, No. 9 (May 1946).

Annotated list of references on the fundamentals of life insurance, its management aspects, and its history. Material for the purchaser included.

"Life Insurance and Personal Economics," *Business Literature.* Newark, N. J., Public Library, Vol. XXVI, No. 3 (November 1953).

Annotated list of books and other references on life insurance from the point of view of the layman, the life underwriter, the trust officer, and the home office.

List of Worthwhile Life Insurance Books. New York, Institute of Life Insurance. Annual.

An annotated list grouped by different types of life insurance source books.

Annuals, handbooks, special compilations

Consolidated Chart of Insurance Organizations. Rochester, *The Fraternal Monitor.* Annual.

Statistical tables for 384 fraternal beneficiary societies, life companies, and life associations.

Crobaugh, C. J., *Handbook of Insurance.* New York, Prentice-Hall, 1949.

Defines more than 5000 terms. Attention is given to the policy analysis, historical development, legal rating, underwriting, statistical, and state control phases of insurance. Includes mortality tables, etc.

Cyclopedia of Insurance in the United States. New York, The Index Publishing Company. Annual.

Contains data on all types of companies, court decisions, definitions, and biographical sketches.

Flitcraft Compend. New York, Flitcraft, Inc. Annual.

Valuable handbook containing general data for all North American companies with more than $100 million of legal-reserve ordinary life insurance, well-known industrial companies, and selected fraternal organizations. Includes comparable data and statistics for U.S. companies with more than $25 million net ordinary life insurance in force.

Insurance Almanac, The; Who, What, When and Where—In Insurance. New York, The Underwriter Printing and Publishing Company. Annual.

Useful information on the insurance business, the officers and directors of all types of companies, insurance department officials, associations, insurance groups, broker's regulatory laws, agents, actuaries, etc.

Life Insurance Fact Book. New York, Institute of Life Insurance. Annual.

A handy reference volume covering the basic facts and figures about the life insurance business as a whole. Statistics start with earliest available, some 1890.

Statistics—Fraternal Societies. Rochester, *The Fraternal Monitor.* Annual.

A manual of statistics covering the records, plans, and rates of most fraternal insurance societies. Includes data on the principal fraternal and secret societies not furnishing insurance as a feature.

Periodicals and services

Best's Insurance News. New York, Best. Weekly.

Has life, fire, and casualty editors. Covers management, office methods, sales and education, and miscellaneous subjects. Company developments appear each month.

Best's Insurance Reports. New York, Best. Annual.

Valuable handbooks containing information on the history, finances, management and operation, officers and directors, and territory where licensed. Critical comments on management and investments.

Best's Life Chart. New York, Best. Annual.

Useful chart showing for each company the number of years in business, principal items of the financial statement, and the cost of insurance at 35 for a period of 10 years.

Best's Life Underwriter's Guide. New York, Best. Annual.

Presents in a compact and easy-to-read style comparative data for the current policy provisions, practices, and types of insurance of 190 large life companies.

Eastern Underwriter. New York. Weekly.

News magazine covering life, fire, marine, casualty, and surety insurance. Carries company news, etc.

Insurance Field. Louisville, Ky. Weekly.

Covers all types of insurance.

National Underwriter, The. Chicago. Weekly.

The national weekly newspaper of insurance. Has life and other than life editions.

Rough Notes. Indianapolis, Ind. Monthly.

Covers casualty and surety insurance fields. Pays special attention to sales methods.

Spectator Compendium of Official Life Insurance Reports. Philadelphia, *The Spectator.* Annual.

Statistical tables showing the business and financial standing of all U.S. life companies. Includes important ratios.

Spectator Handy Guide, The. Philadelphia, *The Spectator.* Annual.

Contains information on standard and special life insurance contracts, nonforfeiture values, and actuarial tables. Primarily useful to the life underwriter.

Spectator Insurance Year Books. Philadelphia, *The Spectator.* Annual.

Useful reference tool, including statistics and information concerning all forms of insurance companies as well as data on foreign companies and business in foreign countries. Critical analysis of the administration of the legal reserve companies.

Directories

New Jersey Insurance Directory. Louisville, Ky., The Insurance Field Company. (Directories for individual states.)

Includes officers, age, financial figures, and agency services of licensed companies, a list of general agents and managers by name and by company, and statistics of individual companies.

General texts

Berman, Edward, *Life Insurance, a Critical Examination.* New York, Harper, 1936.

For the layman in examining life insurance companies.

Huebner, S. S., *Life Insurance.* New York, Appleton, Century, Crofts, 1950.

One of the best-known textbooks on the fundamentals of life insurance.

Ilse, Louise W., *Group Insurance and Employee Retirement Plans.* New York, Prentice-Hall, 1953.

Historical and social backgrounds emphasized.

Kelsey, R. Wilfred and Daniels, Arthur C., *Handbook of Life Insurance.* New York, Institute of Life Insurance, 1953.

An excellent though brief introduction to the fundamentals of life insurance.

McCahan, David, ed., *Accident and Sickness Insurance.* Philadelphia, University of Pennsylvania Press, 1954.

A comprehensive study covering the various health care coverages as well as insurance coverages for replacement of income lost through disability. Though Blue Cross and Blue Shield are included, major emphasis is on insurance companies.

Maclean, J. B., *Life Insurance.* New York, McGraw-Hill, 1951.

A standard text that explains the theory and practice of all branches of life insurance.

Magee, J. H., *General Insurance.* Chicago, Irwin, 1953.

Basic study of general insurance, designed to familiarize the student with insurance fundamentals and coverages plus elementary planning and management.

Mowbray, Albert H., *Insurance; Its Theory and Practice in the United States.* New York, McGraw-Hill, 1946.

A well-organized book covering all types of insurance contracts and insurance carriers, the insurance market, state supervision, and the role of insurance in state policy. Appendix includes a bibliography and many illustrations of insurance contracts, clauses, and forms.

Real Estate and Construction

Bibliographies

"Real Estate Market Today," *Business Literature.* Newark, N. J., Public Library, Vol. XX, No. 2 (October 1947).

An annotated list of references for the buyer as well as the real estate agent, covering appraisal and valuation principles and practices and real estate as a vocation.

"Rehabilitation and Other Real Estate Trends Today," *Business Literature.* Newark, N. J., Public Library, Vol. XXVI, No. 2 (October 1953).

Descriptive list of books, magazine articles, and special reports on urban rehabilitation and trends in real estate development.

"Shopping Centers and Their Effect on Urban Redevelopment," *Business Information Sources.* Cleveland, Ohio, Public Library, Vol. XXV, No. 3 (September-November 1954).

An annotated list of books, periodical articles, and special reports on their development and results.

"Statistical Data for Community Appraisal," *Business Literature.* Newark, N. J., Public Library, Vol. XXIV, No. 8 (April 1952).

A brief list of the special tools for community appraisal, with an introductory statement on their application.

Annuals, handbooks, special compilations

"Annual Report and Forecast," *Engineering News-Record.* New York. February issue.

Predicts construction activity during current year. Provides graphs showing amount of contract awards for each state and for the differing types of construction. Includes data on costs, employment, and related material.

"Construction Costs," *Engineering News-Record.* Annually in October.

Collection of cost indexes important to the construction field. Nationwide and principal city cost indexes are presented, as well as indexes for materials and for different types of construction.

McMichael, S. L., *McMichael's Appraising Manual.* New York, Prentice-Hall, 1951.

After presenting the economic, financial, and social data necessary to an appraiser, the author follows by detailing the technique involved in appraising various types of property. Tables, forms, and bibliography included.

Real Estate Handbook, Holmes, L. G. and Jones, C. M., ed. New York, Prentice-Hall, 1948.

Explains performance of every kind of real estate transaction. Replete with forms and tables. Includes a dictionary of terms.

Periodicals and services

American Builder. Chicago. Monthly.

Over-all information for industry. Many pictures and plans of houses. Helpful ideas for builders.

Appraisal Journal, The. Chicago, American Institute of Real Estate Appraisers of the National Association of Real Estate Boards. Quarterly.

Contains authoritative material on various aspects of appraisal practice and procedure. Excellent signed book reviews.

Advance Building Information. New York, Brown's Letters, Inc.

Daily mimeographed news sheets on building construction in New York area. Lists project, owner, architect, and dates bids close. Reports contracts awarded, and other building data.

Building Supply News. Chicago. Monthly.

Trade conditions, practical suggestions in connection with building materials and merchandising. Price data.

Buildings. Cedar Rapids, Iowa. Monthly.

Comprehensive discussion for those who construct, equip, and maintain office, apartment, and other large buildings.

Dodge Reports. New York, F. W. Dodge. Daily.

A confidential construction news service covering building and engineering projects by counties, states, and established trading areas.

Engineering News-Record. New York. Weekly.

Established authority on construction; has building news section, official proposals, current prices of materials, etc.

Housing Letter. New York, Housing Institute.

A fortnightly interpretive news digest of housing trends and opportunities. Simple and clear in style and keyed to small broker, landlord, and tenant experience rather than broad economic phases.

Land Economics. Madison, Wis., University of Wisconsin. Quarterly.

Contains scholarly articles on planning, housing, and public utilities. Includes book reviews.

Mortgage Banker. Chicago, Mortgage Bankers Association of America. Monthly.

Official organ of the Association, covering current topics of interest in this field. Includes a good statistical section.

National Real Estate and Building Journal. Cedar Rapids, Iowa. Monthly.

Covers current trends in the real estate field for builders, property managers, and real estate brokers.

Real Estate Analyst. St. Louis, Roy Wenzlick & Company.

A comprehensive service on real estate in its broad economic aspects. Statistical material, charts, and graphs support deductions and comment. Construction, rent, and other data in great detail provided on national basis for many areas. Valuable in study of general economic problems as well as for real estate outlook.

Savings and Loan News. Rockford, Ill., U.S. Savings and Loan League. Monthly.

Presents timely articles of interest to savings and loan officials, facts and figures on savings and loan associations, business and real estate trends, and related topics.

Directories

Contractors Register. Sub-Contractors Register, Inc., New York. Annual.

Geographical list of contractors, architects, and engineers in the New York metropolitan area, part of New England, and Florida. Classified list of materials and equipment.

Roster of Realtors, National Real Estate and Building Journal. Cedar Rapids, Iowa. Annual.

Geographical list of members of the National Association of Real Estate Boards, with officers and state officials.

Sweet's Catalogue Service, Inc. Annual.

Alphabetical and geographical list of manufacturers of building materials. Lists products and trade names. Seven volumes of trade catalogs.

General texts

American Institute of Real Estate Appraisers, *The Appraisal of Real Estate.* Chicago, 1951.

Designed for use as a text and reference book, it outlines the essential theories and principles of real estate.

Benson, P. A. and North, N. L., *Real Estate Principles and Practices.* New York, Prentice-Hall, 1947.

Readable text giving the facts about real property ownership and the principal commercial and financial transactions involved in such ownership. Valuable for all engaged in selling, buying, or financing real estate. Gives detailed information on the real estate market, its financing and legal processes, and discusses its relation to the national economy.

Bliss, H. L. and Sill, C. H., *Real Estate Management.* New York, Prentice-Hall, 1953.

Discusses the practical aspects of managing property from the analysis of market and neighborhood conditions to records and controls, relationship with tenants, and details of upkeep.

Holmes, W. G., *Plant Location.* New York, McGraw-Hill, 1930.

Considers the factors involved in choosing the general territory, the particular community, and the site of a plant.

May, A. A., *The Valuation of Residential Real Estate.* New York, Prentice-Hall, 1953.

One of the basic books of appraisal literature. A "how-to-do-it" book.

National Association of Real Estate Boards, *A Primer on Rehabilitation under Local Law Enforcement.* Washington, 1952.

Practical manual embodying the early experience of those communities that have pioneered in wholesale, impartial, and systematic enforcement of ordinances outlawing substandard housing. Summarizes progress in urban conservation.

Woodbury, Coleman, ed., *Urban Redevelopment: Problems and Practices.* Chicago, University of Chicago Press, 1953.

The second volume produced by the Urban Redevelopment Study deals with the major operating problems and practices in local redevelopment programs.

Woodbury, Coleman, ed., *The Future of Cities and Urban Redevelopment.* Chicago, University of Chicago Press, 1953.

A comprehensive study of urban redevelopment, including a thorough analysis of the underlying factors in urban growth and development and of desirable objectives.

Foreign Trade

Bibliographies

"Question of Foreign Trade," *Business Literature.* Newark, N.J., Public Library, Vol. XVIII, No. 5 (January 1946).

Annotated bibliography divided into material on economic problems, market data, sources for information, and trade practices.

"World Trade," *Business Information Sources.* Cleveland, Ohio, Public Library, Vol. XIX, No. 2, Part I-II (May 1948).

Annotated list of books, pamphlets, magazine articles, etc., on training and procedure for foreign trade with related material, and including information on foreign trade organizations.

"World Trade, 1953," *Business Information Sources.* Cleveland, Ohio, Public Library, Vol. XXIV, No. 3 (May-June 1953).

A supplement to an earlier annotated bibliography, emphasizing changing points of view.

Annuals, handbooks, special compilations

Custom House Guide. New York, Import Publications, Inc. Annual.

General port information, import commodity index, U.S. Customs Tariff Act, U.S. Customs regulations, and Internal Revenue Code. Port information includes description and limits, officials, port charges, etc.

Exporters' Encyclopedia. New York, Ashwell. Annual.

Gives shipping regulations, consulates, ports, steamship lines, and American and foreign trade organizations.

Foreign Commerce Yearbook. Washington, U.S. Dept. Commerce. Annual.

Geographical arrangement giving under each country general data, production, transportation, with tables on foreign trade. Section of statistics on international trade; with weights and index.

Pratt, E. E., *Foreign Trade Handbook.* Chicago, Dartnell, 1949.

Aimed primarily at the manufacturer and producer considering the organization of an export department, it gives in detail a complete picture of the background and present status of foreign trade, the management of the department, financial aspects, services available, technical procedures, and other important aspects of foreign trade.

Periodicals

American Import and Export Bulletin. New York. Monthly.

Comprehensive coverage of activities of Bureau of Customs, foreign trade program of Department of Commerce and other government agencies, along with specific information on freight forwarding and other phases of foreign trade.

Export Trade and Shipper. New York. Weekly.

Covers market and credit conditions abroad, problems of export packing and shipping, and political and economic trends affecting foreign trade.

Foreign Commerce Weekly. Washington, U.S. Dept. Commerce. Weekly.

Current foreign trade news, both by countries and by commodities. Regular departments cover new world trade leads, statistical decisions, Latin American and European exchange rates, utilities, and communications.

Directories

Buyers for Export. New York, Ashwell, 1954.

Export merchants, commission houses, manufacturing, and purchasing agents for foreign companies. Also list of export managers with companies they represent.

Kelly's Directory of Merchants, Manufacturers and Shippers. London, Kelly's Directories, Ltd. Annual.

List of merchants, manufacturers, shippers, exporters, importers, commission agents, etc. Geographical arrangement with classified trade sections under each country. Trade index and country and town index covering all countries.

Marconi's International Register. New York, Telegraphic Cable and Radio Registration, Inc. Annual.

An alphabetical list of the principal firms of the world having international contacts, giving both cable and postal addresses as well as the particulars of their business. Classified trades section serves as an international buyers guide.

United States Citizens in World Affairs. New York, Foreign Policy Association, Inc., 1953.

Directory of national organizations concerned with international affairs, and international agencies with headquarters in U.S. Alphabetical list gives executives, objectives, membership, etc. Includes foreign diplomatic and information services, and chambers of commerce in New York City.

General texts

Channels for Trading Abroad. Washington, U.S. Dept. Commerce, 1946.

Valuable to businessmen interested in the field of exporting or importing, either to begin or expand their business. Gives channels for foreign trade, suggests methods of procedure, and describes government services available.

Export and Import Practice. Washington, U.S. Dept. Commerce, 1938.

Techniques of export and import selling described step by step. Especially good for those entering this field for the first time.

Guides for New World Traders. Washington, U.S. Dept. Commerce, 1949.

A compact booklet giving introduction to problems and possibilities in foreign trade. Indicates services in this field by the Department. Includes selected list of other information sources.

Heck, H. J., *Foreign Commerce.* New York, McGraw-Hill, 1953.

An integration into one volume of practical and theoretical aspects of international economics. Forms and a bibliography make up the appendices.

Horn, P. V., *International Trade—Principles and Practices.* New York, Prentice-Hall, 1945.

Readable text giving a complete picture of world trade, both its broad historical and economic aspects and its practical problems for the individual organization.

Huebner, G. G. and Kramer, R. L., *Foreign Trade: Principles and Practices.* New York, Appleton, 1942.

Good standard textbook on general principles, of international commerce, promotion of foreign trade, trading organizations, and methods and financial practices.

Modern Export Packing. Washington, U.S. Dept. Commerce, 1940.

Describes the basic principles of packing export merchandise. Discusses construction and types of containers and gives packing methods for many individual items under the various commodity groups.

Modern Ship Stowage; Including Methods of Handling Cargo at Ocean Terminals. Washington, U.S. Dept. Commerce, 1942.

A comprehensive manual describing present-day cargo handling and stowage methods. Includes suggestions for safer handling and carriage of many commodities that move in international trade. Includes weights and measures used in shipping and also carriage of goods for American and some foreign countries by Sea Acts.

Shaterian, W. S., *Export-Import Banking.* New York, Ronald, 1947.

Deals with the instruments and operations used in financing foreign trade, describes the evolution of foreign banking and the operations of the department. Valuable reference book for importers and exporters for its detailed definitions of terms and processes. Includes sample forms.

Public Utilities, Including Transportation

Annuals

American Gas Association Bureau of Statistics, *Gas Facts, a Statistical Record of the Gas Utility Industry.* New York. Annual.

Discussion and statistics on such phases of the industry as energy reserves, production, distribution, storage, sales and utilization, finance, etc.

Edison Electric Institute, *Electric Utility Industry in the United States.* New York. Annual.

After a summary of the year's operations, this bulletin presents tables, charts, and graphs on the important aspects of the industry. Statistics start with 1920 and continue to the year preceding publication.

Market Guide to Railroads. Chicago, *Modern Railroads.* Annual.

Lists mileage, equipment, personnel, and related data.

Statistics of Railways in the United States. Washington, U.S. Interstate Commerce Commission. Annual.

Based chiefly on the annual reports of steam railways, it presents data on railway and track equipment, traffic, employees, fuel, accidents, revenues, other financial information. Similar statistics are also given for other carriers such as oil pipe lines, electric railways, carriers by water, etc.

Periodicals

Air Transportation. New York. Monthly.

Covers the air cargo industry, including air shipping rates, material handling, cargo plane and terminal development, etc.

American Gas Association Monthly. New York, American Gas Association. Monthly.

Features gas company promotion, government relations, and industry development.

Distribution Age. Philadelphia. Monthly.

Covers shipping, hauling, warehousing, and feature articles on distribution costs, packing for shipment, developments in handling and loading, warehouse design, and other problems in this service industry.

Electrical World. New York. Monthly.

Articles cover management problems, new equipment, construction, etc., as well as news of the field.

Fortnightly Telephone Engineer. Chicago. Monthly.

Deals with management and engineering problems of independent telephone companies primarily.

Gas Age. New York. Semimonthly.

Devoted to operation and management of gas supply facilities.

Mass Transportation. Chicago. Monthly.

Deals with the transit industry, with lengthy articles on bus management. Some short news departments.

Modern Railroads. Chicago. Monthly.

Emphasizes developments for improvement of railroads and their management.

Public Utilities Fortnightly. Washington. Biweekly.

General articles on public utility problems. Regular departments are devoted to progress of regulation and other legal and legislative developments.

Railway Age. New York. Weekly.

Articles on railroad equipment, operation, and finance. A helpful source for financial and operating statistics on the railroad industry.

Shipping Digest. New York. Weekly.

Covers trends, developments, and activities within the shipping industry.

Telephony. Chicago. Monthly.

Treats all phases of telephone company management, new developments, and general news.

Traffic World. Washington. Weekly.

Covers general transportation news and devotes special attention to regulatory action affecting carriers.

Directories

American Aviation World Wide Directory. Washington, American Aviation Publications. Annual.

Alphabetical index of companies in the United States and Canada, Latin America, Africa, Europe, and Australia; manufacturers of aircraft, engines, and equipment.

Brown's Directory of American Gas Companies. New York, Moore. Annual.

Alphabetical index and geographical list of companies in the U.S. and Canada, giving officials, production details, prices, etc.

Lloyd's Register of Shipping. London. Annual.

Lists merchant vessels of the world, giving details of ownership, classification, equipment, etc. Includes list of ships with refrigerating appliances, refrigerated stores; also list of shipowners and managers.

McGraw-Hill Directory of Electric Utilities. New York, McGraw-Hill. Annual.

Geographical list of electric light and power companies in the United States, its possessions, and Canada, giving officers, equipment, and distributors. Includes company index. List of national and state associations, etc.

Mass Transportation's Directory. Chicago, *Mass Transportation.* Annual.

Useful for information about the transit industry. Includes data on manufacturers and suppliers, associations, industry statistics, and operating companies that provide city, suburban, and intercity service.

Motor Freight Directory. Chicago, Leonard. Issued in January and July.

Lists of motor freight carriers published for different areas. Also geographical list by states of towns served by carriers from large cities.

Official Airline Guide. Washington, American Aviation Publications. Monthly.

Contains a wealth of information useful to air passengers. Includes an index to lines, an index to cities served, timetables, maps, mileage information, air express and freight data, postal and travel information, as well as many other important facts.

Official Guide of the Railways and Steam Navigation Lines of the United States, Porto Rico, Canada, Mexico, and Cuba. New York, National Railway Publishing Company. Monthly.

Includes maps, timetables, and a list of stations which shows on what line a given place may be located.

Telephony's Directory of the Telephone Industry. Chicago. Annual.

Directory of American Telephone & Telegraph Company, associated Bell Telephone companies, and independent telephone operating companies by state. Includes much related information.

General texts

Bauer, John and Costello, Peter, *Transforming Public Utility Regulation.* New York, Harper, 1949.

"Presents a needed pattern of regulation and public utility organization if the prevalent system of private ownership and operation is maintained." Preface.

Baum, R. D., *Federal Power Commission and State Utility Regulation.* Washington, American Council on Public Affairs, 1943.

An informative and complete report on the procedures and experiences of Power Commission administration.

Bonbright, J. C., *Public Utilities and the National Power Policies.* New York, Columbia University Press, 1940.

A brief, well-balanced interpretation of recent developments in the electric power field.

Electric Power and Government Policy. New York, Twentieth Century Fund, 1948.

Designed to give an objective, factual picture of the industry in relation to government agencies.

Fair, M. L., *Economics of Transportation.* New York, Harper, 1950.

Shows the plan of transportation in the flow of utilities making up the American economic system. Deals with rail, air, water, highway, and pipeline transportation in terms of development, service, rates, regulation, and policy.

Locklin, D. P., *Economics of Transportation.* Chicago, Irwin, 1954.

Using railroad transportation as a basis for comparison, this is treated at length throughout, though not at the expense of other modes of transport. Water transportation is given two chapters, highway transportation four, air transportation two, and pipelines one.

Thompson, C. W., *Public Utility Economics.* New York, McGraw-Hill, 1941.

An excellent text that shows the impact of the Roosevelt administration on the industry and relates public utility economics to the whole economic system.

Westmeyer, R. E., *Economics of Transportation.* New York, Prentice-Hall, 1952.

Detailed discussion of railroad, highway, air, water, pipeline, and other forms of transportation.

chapter XII

Business Organization and Administration

Corporation management. Personnel and industrial relations. Accounting. Office aids. Small business.

CORPORATION MANAGEMENT

Bibliographies

"Corporation Finance," *Business Literature.* Newark, N.J., Public Library, Vol. XXII, No. 4 (December 1949).

Descriptive bibliography of books and special reports on the financial policies of corporations and their relation to management problems.

"Executive Development," *Business Information Sources.* Cleveland, Ohio, Public Library, Vol. XXIII, No. 3 (July-September 1952).

An annotated bibliography of books, pamphlets, and magazine articles covering the many phases of this subject.

Executive Development (Reference list No. 11, April, 1952), P. H. Myren, compiler. Cambridge, Mass., Harvard University, Graduate School of Business Administration, 1952.

A selected list of books, pamphlets, and articles published since 1935.

"Management and Its Many Aspects," *Business Literature.* Newark, N.J., Public Library, Vol. XXI, No. 8 (April 1949).

Descriptive list of references to books and pamphlets on the functions and procedures involved in management.

"Reading for Supervisory Training," *Business Literature*. Newark, N.J., Public Library, Vol. XXVI, No. 1 (September 1953).

Annotated bibliography of books dealing with supervision at different levels.

Annuals, handbooks, special compilations

Brown, S. M. and Doris, Lillian, eds., *Business Executive's Handbook*. New York, Prentice-Hall, 1953.

A volume specially designed to provide answers to management problems whether they relate to selling, advertising, insurance, office management, or credit and collectors. Tables and forms are included, as well as a glossary of abbreviations and a detailed index.

Donald, W. J., ed., *Handbook of Business Administration*. New York, McGraw-Hill, 1931.

Presents in convenient form the fundamentals and procedures of managerial policy and technique.

Dooher, M. J., *Development of Executive Talent: A Handbook of Management Development Techniques and Case Studies*. New York, American Management Association, 1952.

Presents principles and tested practices underlying sound executive training and management, prepared by forty-four recognized authorities in this field. Includes an appendix of forms and a bibliography.

Rice, J. O., ed., *The Management Leader's Manual*. New York, American Management Association, 1947.

Twenty-two essays on various facets of management are grouped under seven major headings. Among the topics—management leadership, responsibilities, interviewing and counseling techniques, safe and efficient production, simplicity, etc.

Periodicals and services

Advanced Management. New York. Quarterly.

Journal of the Society for the Advancement of Management. Book reviews and authoritative articles on specialized phases.

American Business. Chicago. Monthly.

General business coverage with special emphasis on office management. Book reviews.

Corporate Director. New York, American Institute of Management. Irregular.

Association publications on management appraisal, industry audits, etc. Analysis of management policies of specific companies as well as of the effect of practices and policies in management.

Credit and Financial Management. New York. Monthly.

Covers financial problems, budgets, collections, sales, business insurance; regular sections devoted to new books, answers to credit questions, etc.

Dun's Review and Modern Industry. New York. Monthly.

Aimed primarily at the executive, this publication attempts to present the most advanced thinking on the problems of executive technique. Articles are on production, supervisory personnel, consumer research, executive training, and the latest factory techniques. The regular departments include information on new methods and materials, views of top management men on current business and community problems, and a detailed picture of the current business trend.

Fortune. New York. Monthly.

A massive, gorgeously illustrated picture of great industrial movements. Thoughtful feature articles, well supplemented by striking photographs or vivid charts on industry or industrial leaders, or developments from science to economics. Opinion surveys carried out in detail a regular feature. Frequent excellent book review articles.

Harvard Business Review. Boston. Bimonthly.

A review on a broad scale, based on university research.

Journal of Business of the University of Chicago. Chicago. Quarterly.

Devoted to the scientific and professional interests of business as approached through a graduate school. Book reviews.

Management Methods. New York. Monthly.

Covers various phases of management with emphasis on office management.

Management News. New York, American Management Association. Monthly.

Devoted largely to the plans and activities of the association. Contains a valuable research article on some phase of management each month.

Management Record. New York, National Industrial Conference Board. Monthly.

Valuable for articles on both management and labor. Contains frequent surveys of company practices, selected labor statistics, the Board's consumer price index, book reviews, and other useful material.

Management Review. New York, American Management Association. Monthly.

Presents articles on industrial relations, office management, production, marketing, finance, etc. Each section has an annotated list of relevant periodical articles. Book reviews.

Nation's Business. Washington. Monthly.

As the organ of established management, reflects its point of view in many interpretative articles on Washington developments, management, labor relations, countrywide economic trends. Regular features include *Management's* Washington letters, book reviews, and short news notes.

Prentice-Hall Corporation Service. New York.

Consists of two loose-leaf supplemented volumes. Volume I is a treatise dealing with law and practice in corporation matters. Volume II is the compilation of laws of a given state with monthly supplements.

Directories

Association of Consulting Management Engineers, Inc., *Membership List.* New York, the Association.

An alphabetical list devoting a full page to each member firm, showing services offered, firm members, and address. Includes the association's code of ethics, purpose of the association, and how to select and use management counsel.

Business Executives of America. New York, Institute for Research in Biography, 1950.

Biographies of living executives of American and Canadian corporations.

Poor's Register of Directors and Executives. New York, Standard & Poor's. Annual.

Alphabetical list of officers and directors in business organizations of the U.S. and Canada. Listings by corporations and individuals. Includes revisionary supplements.

Who's Who in Commerce and Industry. Chicago, Marquis, 1953.

Alphabetical sketches of executives and others noteworthy in commerce and industry in the United States, Canada, and foreign countries. Name index.

General texts

Argyris, Chris, *Executive Leadership.* New York, Harper, 1953.

An appraisal of the work of an industrial executive from several points of view, including those directed.

Bowen, H. R., *Social Responsibilities of the Businessman.* New York, Harper, 1953.

The third volume of a study of Christian ethics and economic life by the National Council of Churches. Includes a bibliography on the businessman's conception of the social responsibilities of business.

Given, W. B. J., *Bottom-up Management.* New York, Harper, 1949.

The philosophy of decentralization of management authority and responsibility, as based on one company's experience.

Guthman, H. G., *Corporate Financial Policy.* New York, Prentice-Hall, 1955.

Management point of view emphasized in relation to the financial policy of corporations. The text includes discussion of problems involved in acquisition of funds and property, and management of corporate net income.

Hempel, E. H., *Top-Management Planning.* New York, Harper, 1946.

Scrutinizes proposals and sets up prerequisites for successful industrial planning. Describes and combines methods into a system usable by giant corporations or small producers.

Martindell, Jackson, *Scientific Appraisal of Management.* New York, Harper, 1950.

Discusses the methods that have been developed by sending management questionnaires and evaluation charts to industries to determine the value of management, beyond the actual returns of invested capital.

Newman, W., *Administrative Action.* New York, Prentice-Hall, 1951.

Dealing with principles and techniques of administration, this book aims to give the executive a better perspective and understanding of his job of administering.

Schell, E. H., *The Technique of Executive Control.* New York, McGraw-Hill, 1950.

An attempt at a constructive analysis of executive conduct and executive straight thinking. Aimed at building an executive method best suited to each personality.

Tead, Ordway, *Art of Administration.* New York, McGraw-Hill, 1951.

Seeks to show how administration can become more effective under the conditions and challenges of American life and what its role should be in a technological society.

Personnel and Industrial Relations

Bibliographies

Barnes, R. M., *Bibliography of Industrial Engineering and Management Literature, 1946.* Dubuque, Iowa, Author, 1946.

Includes most of the important books in the field of industrial engineering and articles and papers on motion study, etc.

"Counseling in Industry," *Business Information Sources.* Cleveland, Ohio, Public Library, Vol. XXII, No. 2 (September-December 1951).

Annotated bibliography on the function of the counselor and his relationship to the organization and to the individual.

Employment Tests in Industry and Business, Hazel Benjamin, compiler. Princeton, N.J., Princeton University, Industrial Relations Section, 1945.

A selected annotated bibliography on this subject. Includes sources of information, publishers, addresses, bibliographies, and author index.

"Industrial Relations, Personnel Administration and Labor Relations," in *Reading List on Business Administration*. Hanover, N.H., Dartmouth College, Amos Tuck School of Business Administration, 1952.

Annotated bibliography of some forty-eight books, supplemented by a list of associations and periodicals in the field.

Office Library of an Industrial Relations Executive. Princeton, N.J., Princeton University, Industrial Relations Section, 1951.

Annotated bibliography helpful to the executive who needs information on problems and policies outside his own experience. Lists books on the economics of employment, wages, and hours, and on the administrative problems and methods of higher management. An additional section on studies, reports, periodicals, commerce and government information services, and research organizations is included.

Personnel Administration: A Selected and Annotated Bibliography, Keith Davis, compiler. Austin, Texas, University of Texas, Bureau of Business Research, 1952.

An excellent comprehensive list of books and periodicals with annotations that not only describe but evaluate the publications noted.

"Personnel Management," *Business Literature*. Newark, N.J., Public Library, Vol. XXII, No. 2-3 (October-November 1949).

Annotated bibliography limited to books published 1947-49. Includes a list of management magazines.

Annuals, handbooks, special compilations

Aspley, J. C., *Handbook of Industrial Relations*. Chicago, Dartnell, 1952.

Presents in handy form the experience, tested methods, views, and practices of companies successful in building sound relationships with their employees.

Benn, A. E., *Management Dictionary*. New York, Exposition Press, 1952.

Contains over 4000 words, formulas, synonyms, and tables currently used in personnel management.

Halsey, G. D., *Handbook of Personnel Management*. New York, Harper, 1953.

Methods in personnel management in organizations of fewer than 3000 employees. Includes outline for a self-audit of personnel management and list of sources of information and help in personnel management. Bibliography at end of each chapter.

Mee, J. F., ed., *Personnel Handbook*. New York, Ronald, 1951.

A compact and practical guide. Includes material on budgets, size of staff, etc., for personnel department for companies of varying size, a section on manpower and cost control, discussion of personnel tests, etc.

Periodicals and services

Personnel. New York, American Management Association. Bimonthly.

Standards in personnel management in all its aspects covered in articles by authorities.

Personnel Journal. New York, Personnel Journal, Inc. Bimonthly.

Contributions by specialists on human factors in management and the adjustment of individuals to their occupations. Book reviews.

General texts

Barnes, R. M., *Motion and Time Study*. New York, Wiley, 1949.

Excellent treatment of the subject with emphasis on motion study principles and procedures. Includes a chapter on training programs.

Given, W. B., Jr., *Reaching Out in Management*. New York, Harper, 1953.

Consideration of the ways in which employees may be helped to find satisfaction in their work and to bring about development of their full potentialities.

Halsey, G. D., *Selecting and Inducting Employees.* New York, Harper, 1951.

A handbook for those who select and induct employees in factories, stores, and offices with emphasis on tests. Includes a suggested library on selection and induction, a list of sources of information, and many sample forms.

Jucius, M. J., *Personnel Management.* Chicago, Irwin, 1948.

The emphasis is upon principles with descriptions of good practice and selected examples of generally accepted solutions to common problems. Illustrations from industry, distribution, and office work.

Laird, D. A. and Laird, E. C., *Technique of Handling People.* New York, McGraw-Hill, 1954.

How to obtain better human relations with others with techniques used by today's successful people; expressed in simple terms, illustrated by many anecdotes.

Pigors, Paul, *Personnel Administration.* New York, McGraw-Hill, 1947.

"Stresses the philosophy of personnel administration instead of giving a detailed analysis of systems and procedures."

Scott, W. D., *Personnel Management.* New York, McGraw-Hill, 1949.

A standard work completely revised; a thorough and well-organized analysis and evaluation of modern practices. Includes extensive bibliography.

Tiffin, Joseph, *Industrial Psychology.* New York, Prentice-Hall, 1952.

Discusses individual differences; the interview; testing mental ability; mechanical aptitude; dexterity; personality, interest, and visual skills; training; inspection; merit rating; wages and job evaluation; work; accidents and safety; and attitudes and morals. Elementary descriptive statistics are considered in the appendix.

Waite, W. W., *Personnel Administration.* New York, Ronald, 1952.

A textbook divided into these four broad divisions: (1) starting a personnel administration program; (2) assembling the force; (3) keeping the force going; (4) dealing with the force. Contains 118 illustrations.

Yoder, Dale, *Personnel Management and Industrial Relations*. New York, Prentice-Hall, 1948.

New edition of basic text contains expanded discussions of several major industrial relation functions, including job analysis, morale measurement and maintenance, job evaluation, and salary administration.

Accounting

Bibliographies

Accountants' Index. New York, American Institute of Accountants, 1921. Supplements 1923-51.

A bibliography of accounting literature in the form of an analytical subject index covering accountancy and many other phases of business.

"Accounting," in *Reading List on Business Administration*. Hanover, N.H., Dartmouth College, Amos Tuck School of Business Administration, 1952.

A descriptive list of some eighty publications on accounting and related subjects divided under the headings of introductory and general principles and methods, accounting theory, financial analysis, controllership, auditing, etc.

"Government and Accounting Today," *Business Literature*. Newark, N.J., Public Library, Vol. XXIV, No. 3 (November 1951).

A descriptive list of periodical and pamphlet references bearing on government contract problems and related subjects.

"Significant Books on Cost Accounting," *Business Literature*. Newark, N.J., Public Library, Vol. XXV, No. 5 (January 1953).

An annotated list of current publications of special value to the cost accountant.

"Suggestions for the Cost Accountants' Bookshelf," *Business Literature*. Newark, N.J., Public Library, Vol. XXVII, No. 6 (February 1955).

Annotated list of books selected for their especial value to the cost accountant from those published 1942-54.

Annuals, handbooks, special compilations

Kohler, E. L., *Dictionary for Accountants.* New York, Prentice-Hall, 1952.

A translation of fundamental accounting terms into words having meaning in other fields.

Lang, Theodore, ed., *Cost Accountant's Handbook.* New York, Ronald, 1949.

Presents the fundamental principles, methods, and techniques of cost accounting, primarily for manufacturing industries. Includes many illustrations.

Lasser, J. K., ed., *Handbook of Accounting Methods.* New York, Van Nostrand, 1940.

Designed for accountants, system designers, and executives, it first presents the techniques of designing an accounting system, next it advises on the records required for tax and other legislation, and lastly it presents the method of accounting used in over one hundred types of business. In the last a brief description of the business is first given; theory of the accounts required and model statements are included. Bibliography.

Lasser, J. K., ed., *Handbook of Cost Accounting Methods.* New York, Van Nostrand, 1949.

Seventy contributors have combined to produce a practical aid to the cost accountant. They first present the background of cost accounting, then the theory and its practical application; finally the systems used by over sixty types of industries and commercial establishments are discussed. The bibliography at the end presents further reading material for those interested in a specific industry.

Lasser, J. K., *Handbook of Tax Accounting Methods.* New York, Van Nostrand, 1951.

A guide to tax accounting practices in various industries. Specific variations from general tax principles as practiced in ninety-six industries are described. There is also a survey of tax principles that will apply to all industries. Contains an extensive bibliography. This book can be used by beginners, professionals, and by the corporate officer or banker.

Paton, W. A., ed., *Accountant's Handbook.* New York, Ronald, 1943.

Presents in compact and digested form, the essential principles, rules, and procedures involved in the entire field of accounting.

Periodicals and services

Accounting Review. Menasha, Wis., American Accounting Association. Quarterly.

Articles contributed by accounting school instructors cover education of accountants, practice and theory of accounting, and improvement of the profession. Detailed reviews of books on accounting, finance, statistics, taxation, etc.

Bulletins. New York, National Association of Cost Accountants. Monthly.

These and other research publications of the association are invaluable sources of information on the general aspects of cost accounting and of its applications to the problems of specific companies.

Controller, The. Brattleboro, Vt., Controllers Institute of America, Inc. Monthly.

Accounting and related topics presented at the executive level. Regular departments include "Washington News," "Paging the New Books," "Dates Ahead," "Personals," and "Opportunities."

Journal of Accountancy. New York, American Institute of Accountants. Monthly.

Includes articles by practicing accountants on the theory, practice, and problems of accounting. Annotated books and articles are a regular feature.

New York Certified Public Accountant. New York, New York State Society of Certified Public Accountants. Monthly.

Contributors are practicing public accountants, discussing problems and developments in their field. While aimed at New Yorkers, the scope of this periodical is of national interest. Book reviews.

General texts

Bradshaw, T. F. and Hull, C. C., eds., *Controllership in Modern Management.* Chicago, Irwin, 1949.

Each chapter is on a distinct phase of controllership, written by an authority in the field. The book is part of a joint project of the Controllers Institute of America and the Controllership Foundation.

Finney, H. A., *Principles of Accounting: Introductory.* New York, Prentice-Hall, 1948.

A basic textbook on the mechanics and principles of accounting, replete with illustrative material. Serves as a basis for the author's intermediate and advanced texts.

Foulke, R. A., *Practical Financial Statement Analysis.* New York, McGraw-Hill, 1950.

A comprehensive study of the problems and methods of balance sheet, profit and loss, and surplus analysis.

Gillespie, Cecil, *Accounting Procedure for Standard Costs.* New York, Ronald, 1952.

Profusely illustrated textbook explaining the three fundamental methods of operating standard costs and illustrating their application by means of four case histories. Includes glossary of terms and problems.

Robnett, R. H. and others. *Accounting; a Management Approach.* Chicago, Irwin, 1951.

Planned for the business student who does not expect to become an accountant but who must use accounting data as a basis for decisions.

Specthrie, S. W., *Basic Cost Accounting.* New York, Prentice-Hall, 1950.

Covers such phases of manufacturing cost accounting as job-lot process and operational cost accounting, cost accounting with the use of standards, cost accounting for residuals, by-products and joint products, and the use of such data in formulating business policy.

Office Aids

Bibliographies

"Desk Library of Information Sources," *Business Literature.* Newark, N.J., Public Library, Vol. XIX, No. 7 (March 1947).

Annotated list of the indexes, lists, and compilations most broadly useful.

Noma Bibliography for Office Management. Philadelphia, National Office Management Association, February 1953.

A classified compilation of references to articles and publications published 1949-52 with concise annotations. Over 1200 items noted. Invaluable for its coverage.

"The Secretary's Reference Kit," *Business Literature*. Newark, N.J., Public Library, Vol. XXI, No. 6 (February 1949).

Reference tools that the efficient secretary should have on her desk. Includes references on secretarial practice, formal usage, office manners, information compilations, and current information.

Annuals, handbooks, special compilations

Hutchinson, L. I., *Standard Handbook for Secretaries*. New York, McGraw-Hill, 1950.

An accepted guide to the details of secretarial responsibilities, from correct forms for any correspondence contingency to broader questions of office policy.

Maze, C. L., *Office Management; A Handbook*. New York, Ronald, 1947.

Based on the contributions of leading authorities and sponsored by the National Office Management Association, this is the leading work in the field. Divided into the organization, human, physical, operation, and control elements.

Measures, Howard, *Styles of Address; a Manual of Usage in Writing and in Speech*. New York, Crowell, 1947.

Shows, in several gradations of formal and friendly style, the form of address and title, the salutation, and the complimentary close in English correspondence with people in different parts of the world, and the style to use in speaking to and in referring to persons in various countries.

Periodicals and services

Office. New York. Monthly.

Emphasizes articles on office equipment, management, and personnel relations. Includes book reviews, data on new products, etc.

Office Executive. Philadelphia. Monthly.

Official publication of the National Office Management Association. Articles on office problems, supplemented by notes on equipment and on association activities.

Office Management. New York. Monthly.

Comprehensive articles on methods, equipment, personnel, and purchasing, supplemented by news paragraphs.

Directories

Who Makes it and Where. New York, Geyer. Annual.

Alphabetical list of manufacturers of office supplies and equipment; classified list of trade names and associations.

General texts

Becker, E. R. and Lawrence, R. L., *Success and Satisfaction in Your Office Job.* New York, Harper, 1954.

How common sense, tact, imagination, and good judgment can be used to bring recognition, appreciation, and advancement brought out clearly in this constructive guide to a successful office career.

Faunce, F. A., *Secretarial Efficiency.* New York, McGraw-Hill, 1948.

A reference book for all secretaries. Provides a background of the business knowledge necessary to intelligent secretarial service. Illustrates short cuts to reduce detail.

Niles, M. C. H., *Middle Management.* New York, Harper, 1949.

Gives special consideration to business organizations where clerical work is a major factor, and highlights the management problems of the junior administrator.

Small Business

General texts

Black, N. H., *How to Organize and Manage a Small Business.* Norman, Okla., University Press, 1950.

Planned to help the new small businessman increase his chances of success by dealing with facts, figures, and plans. The appendix includes an outline for a market survey plus a checklist for new business and planning.

Holtzman, R. S. and Livingston, A. K., eds., *Big Business Methods for the Small Business.* New York, Harper, 1952.

Makes available to small businessmen the information and guidance usually available to the largest corporations. Each chapter written by an authority in his field. Bibliography.

Kahm, H. S., *Small Business of Your Own.* New York, Knickerbocker, 1945.

Shows the various fields available for the individual with $100 to $2000 of capital to invest.

Kelley, P. C. and Lawyer, Kenneth, *How to Organize and Operate a Small Business.* New York, Prentice-Hall, 1949.

Discusses each important management function, pointing out variations in application in the fields of merchandising, manufacturing, and service businesses. Extensive bibliography.

Lasser, J. K., *How to Run a Small Business.* New York, McGraw-Hill, 1950.

A guide and checklist for all small businessmen. Includes separate chapters on operating a store efficiently, operating a plant profitably, making profits in wholesaling, and operating a business office most efficiently. Bibliography.

Management Aids for the Small Business. Washington, Small Business Administration, U.S. Dept. Commerce.

Technical aids for the small business.

Small Business Manuals. Washington, U.S. Dept. Commerce.

A series of pamphlets on "establishing and operating a variety of business enterprises," discussing problems of location, financing, advertising, store layout, record keeping, etc. While outdated, they contain still useful data.

Small Business Series. New York State, Dept. Commerce. 10 parts. 1945 or 1946.

Ten bulletins designed to aid in establishment and successful management of New York State small businesses. Financial services, choosing a location, purchasing, inventory control, and record keeping are among the topics covered.

chapter XIII

Industrial Production

Plant Management. Basic Industries.

Plant Management

Bibliographies

"Aids to Industrial Purchasing," *Business Literature.* Newark, N. J., Public Library, Vol. XXVII, No. 7 (March 1955).

Annotated bibliography of books and magazine articles on inventory control, cost reduction, etc.

"Automation," *Business Information Sources.* Cleveland, Ohio, Public Library, Vol. XXIV, No. 4 (July-December 1953).

An extensive annotated bibliography on what automation is and its effect on industrial development.

"Industrial Directories," *Business Information Sources.* Cleveland, Ohio, Public Library, Vol. XXIII, No. 5 (November 1952).

Descriptive list of state industrial directories.

"Materials Handling," *Business Information Sources.* Cleveland, Ohio, Public Library, Vol. XXIV, No. 2 (April 1953).

Series of references on manuals for materials handling, needed equipment, plant layout, etc.

Outstanding Books on Industrial Relations. Princeton, N. J., Princeton University, Industrial Relations Section. Annual.

An annotated list of the important publications for each year.

"State Industrial Directories," *Business Literature.* Newark, N. J., Public Library, Vol. XXIV, No. 7 (March 1952).

Annotated list showing wide diversity in these publications and indicating coverage on such points as number of employees, products, names of officers, and economic data.

Thole, H. C., *Management Controls.* Kalamazoo, Mich., Upjohn Institute, 1953.

An annotated bibliography of books, magazine articles, and other materials on organization for control, needed tools, and methods of appraising results.

Annuals, handbooks, special compilations

Alford, L. P. and Bangs, J. R., eds., *Production Handbook.* New York, Ronald, 1944.

Deals with problems of men, materials, and machines. Discusses plant organization and layout; wage plans, factory budgets; time study and operation analysis.

Brady, G. S., *Materials Handbook.* New York, McGraw-Hill, 1951.

An encyclopedia for purchasing agents, engineers, executives, and foremen. Contains basic data on all kinds of industrial materials and their uses.

Census of Manufactures. Washington, U.S. Dept. Commerce, Bur. Census. Quintennial. 3 vols.

Employment and payrolls, size of establishment, type of organization, inventories, and expenditures for plant and equipment are among the subjects for which statistics are available. Volume I contains a general summary, Volume II contains statistics by industry, and Volume III contains statistics by state.

Commodity Yearbook. New York, Commodity Research Bureau. Annual.

Brief descriptions of commodities from alcohol to zinc, along with notes on their uses, are followed by tables on production, consumption, prices, etc. Both world and United States figures are given.

Market Data Book Number. Industrial Marketing, Chicago. Annual.

Contains basic data on industrial and trade markets and the business magazines and directories serving these markets. Includes many statistical tables and data on industrial development, indicating sources for further investigation. Gives format details and total circulation. Information supplemented by descriptive advertisements.

Periodicals and services

American Machinist. New York. Semimonthly.

The magazine of metal-working production with feature articles in the fields of administration, engineering, tooling, material handling, cutting, and forming. Regular departments include shop equipment news, new books, round-table discussion, and general news of the industry.

Factory Management and Maintenance. New York. Monthly.

The comprehensive magazine in its field. Authoritative articles on all phases of production maintenance and labor management. Includes results and deductions from many special surveys. Regular departments include book reviews and notes on industrial films.

Industrial Equipment News. New York. Monthly.

Devoted to news of tools and new equipment for the industrial world. Materials and supplies covered also.

Mill and Factory. New York. Monthly.

"Industry's know-how magazine of management, maintenance, and production." Trade notes, production methods, and new equipment. Trade literature.

Purchasing. New York. Monthly.

Current information on purchasing for industry and government; for executives in this important field of management. Commodity prices.

Directories

Conover-Mast Purchasing Directory. New York, Conover-Mast. Annual.

Classified lists of manufacturers of industrial equipment, products, and materials. Includes trade name section, also address section in a separate supplement.

Directory of New England Manufacturers. Boston, Hall. Annual.

An excellent example of a regional industrial directory. Covers all New England, arranged geographically and alphabetically by firm and by product. Gives names of officers, types of product, and number employed. Includes brand name section.

Industrial Research Laboratories of the United States. Washington, National Research Council, 1950.

Descriptive listing of nearly 3000 laboratories, indicating personnel and outlining research activities and resources. Includes subject and geographic indexes.

MacRae's Blue Book. Chicago, MacRae's Blue Book Co. Annual.

An A-to-Z list of industrial manufacturers. Includes advertisers and their distributors in boldface type, together with their addresses. Nonadvertisers are listed only under home office address. Capital ratings given.

Thomas' Register of American Manufacturers. New York, Thomas. Annual.

A directory classifying manufacturers by product but including both an alphabetical list and a trade name index. Closely indexed. An invaluable guide to industrial development.

General texts

Bethel, L. L. and others, *Industrial Organization and Management.* New York, McGraw-Hill, 1950.

Emphasis is given to interdependence of all functions of an enterprise. Significant developments in labor and governmental influence in relation to management of industry are observed.

Davis, R. C., *Industrial Organization and Management.* New York, Harper, 1940.

Excellent text including extensive presentation of fundamentals, followed by detailed treatment of plant location, purchasing, office and personnel management.

Fabricant, Solomon, *The Output of Manufacturing Industries, 1899-1937.* New York, National Bureau of Economic Research, 1940.

The first of several reports dealing with the trends of production and productivity in American industry since the beginning of the twentieth century. Valuable statistical tables included.

Heinritz, S. F., *Purchasing.* New York, Prentice-Hall, 1951.

An excellent book on industrial purchasing defining principles, procedures and policies by the editor of *Purchasing* magazine.

Spriegel, W. R. and Lansburgh, R. H., *Industrial Management.* New York, Wiley, 1947.

Outlines the history of industrial management and treats industry's fundamental conditions, organization structure, plant and equipment, motion and time study, wages, buying, selling, and transportation, material and production control, and industrial relations. Appendix includes details of standard nomenclature and a bibliography.

BASIC INDUSTRIES

Bibliographies

Epples, J. D., "List of Resources on Leather," *Journal of Retailing.* New York, Winter 1950.

An excellent descriptive list grouped by subject with introductory comment on the general aspect.

Metals Industries in Texas. Austin, University of Texas Bureau of Business Research, 1952.

A selected annotated bibliography of references that are useful, notwithstanding the limitation in coverage.

Annuals, handbooks, special compilations

AUTOMOTIVE INDUSTRY

Automotive Industries, Annual Statistical Number. Philadelphia. March issue.

Although devoted primarily to providing information on motor vehicles, it also gives data on the aviation and automotive engine industries and on production, materials, and management as they affect these industries.

CHEMICAL INDUSTRY

Chemical Industry Facts Book. Washington, Manufacturing Chemists Association, 1953.

A collection of current facts and general information about the industry.

Haynes, Williams, *Chemical Trade Names and Commercial Synonyms.* New York, Van Nostrand, 1951.

A dictionary of American usage.

Perry, J. H., ed., *Chemical Business Handbook.* New York, McGraw-Hill, 1954.

Prepared by a staff of specialists and covers such topics as finance, research, production, sales, patents, etc. Bibliography and tables included.

METAL INDUSTRY

American Iron and Steel Institute Statistical Report. New York. Annual.

Statistics for the industry on production, employment, capacity, consumption of raw materials, and shipments of products.

Iron Age, Annual Review and Forecast. Philadelphia. January issue.

Data on the important phases of the capital goods industry such as production, metals, and materials, followed by tables, charts, and graphs showing prices, production, capacity, and financial figures for the steel, nonferrous, pig iron, ore, and related industries.

"Metal Statistics," *American Metal Market.* New York. Annual.

Statistical information on ferrous and nonferrous metals, including mining, production, prices, consumption, export-import, etc., figures.

PETROLEUM INDUSTRY

Petroleum Facts and Figures. New York, American Petroleum Institute. Biennial.

Tables of figures, many with state breakdowns, on all aspects of the industry: utilization, production, refining, transportation, prices, and taxation. Includes related material on labor, safety, financial statistics, etc.

Statistical Bulletin. New York, American Petroleum Institute. Annual.

A detailed picture of the growth of the petroleum industry, beginning with 1918. Statistics cover production and consumption, including regional breakdown, exports, imports, and stocks of crude oil and refined products.

TEXTILE INDUSTRY

Textile Organon Review. New York, Textile Economics Bureau. Annual.

Covers statistics and graphs on world and United States production and consumption of man-made fibers, particularly rayon and acetate. Imports and exports, shipments, prices, and consumption figures are also included.

Periodicals and services

AUTOMOTIVE INDUSTRY

Automotive Industries. Philadelphia. Semimonthly.

Technical progress noted, along with production and management phases. Statistical data, convention dates included. Standard authority.

Automotive News. Detroit. Weekly.

Articles on manufacturing, selling, servicing. Features the management level.

Motor. New York. Monthly.

Emphasizes service operation and management problems. Covers news of the field.

CHEMICAL AND DRUG INDUSTRY

Chemical and Engineering News. Washington. Weekly.

Current news of developments in the chemical process industries, including business and finance as well as new products.

Chemical Week. New York. Weekly.

Serves management in the chemical industry. Departments include "Production," "Distribution," "Business and Industry," "Markets," "Research," etc.

Drug and Cosmetic Industry. New York. Monthly.

Treats manufacturing end of industry. Latest ideas on advertising and selling, and packaging. Regular departments devoted to patents, abstracts, raw material prices.

Drug Topics. New York. Monthly.

Current developments on buying and selling for retail stores. Helpful ideas, news notes, lists of sources of supply for the retailer.

Industrial and Engineering Chemistry. Washington. Monthly.

Articles planned for manufacturing, plant, and research executives. Departments include "Plant Management," "Materials Handling," "Industrial Waste," etc.

Modern Plastics. New York. Monthly.

For the entire industry from processors to users, covering latest developments in products and techniques.

Oil, Paint and Drug Reporter. New York. Weekly.

Treats technical aspects. Gives prices of chemicals, dyestuffs, drugs, paints, oils, and fertilizers.

Plastics World. Greenwich, Conn. Monthly.

Emphasizes new equipment and materials and their applications in the plastic industry.

ELECTRICAL INDUSTRY

Electrical Manufacturing. New York. Monthly.

Covers problems of design and production, marketing, administration, and rebuilding. Patents, business news.

Electrical Merchandising. New York. Monthly.

Emphasis is on retail level of distribution. Sales problems, growth of industry, new products covered. Statistical comment.

Electrical World. New York. Weekly.

Articles for the electrical manufacturer. Includes statistical features, trade notes, technical developments. Some book reviews.

Power. New York. Monthly.

Covers power generators and transmissions of all types. Reports production and marketing of supplies, material, and products.

FOOD INDUSTRY

American Restaurant Magazine. Chicago. Monthly.

Covers employee training, merchandising, and management. Food recipes and ideas, etc. Cost charts well illustrated. Trade comment. Equipment notes.

Chain Store Age. New York. Monthly.

Management, price maintenance, etc. Construction and equipment notes. Financial, statistical, and real estate sections, showing new stores and locations.

Food Buyer. New York. Monthly.

Covers all angles of food industry but puts special attention on purchasing and marketing aspects.

Food Engineering. New York. Monthly.

Covers all aspects of industry, stressing cost cutting and quality improvement. Includes new processes, construction, maintenance, equipment, and activities of special companies in food manufacturing industry.

Food Processing. Chicago. Monthly.

Covers processing developments and controls, material handling, packaging, etc.

Food Topics. New York. Semimonthly.

Covers the food field with special attention to retailers. Sections include "Store Engineering and Equipment," "Promotion Aids and Merchandising," etc.

Fountain and Fast Food Service. New York. Monthly.

Merchandising and management for luncheonettes, drive-ins, fountains, snack bars, etc. Covers promotion, personnel management, etc.

Frozen Food Age. New York. Monthly.

Planned for the retailer and covering display, management, etc.

Restaurant Management. New York. Monthly.

Covers restaurant and tea room operation, maintenance. Shows trends in the industry, new equipment; and reviews books of interest to managers and executives. Menu suggestions.

LEATHER INDUSTRY

Boot and Shoe Recorder. New York. Semimonthly.

Emphasis is on the retail end of shoe business. Regular departments include manufacturing and markets.

Leather and Shoes. Boston. Weekly.

Covers the leather and shoe manufacturing industry from factory operation and processing to merchandising and markets.

Luggage & Leather Goods. New York. Monthly.

Covers all angles of the leather goods business for retailers. Stresses sales training, display, and other sales-building techniques.

METAL AND MINING INDUSTRY

American Metal Market. New York. Daily.

The market authority, containing daily reports and closing prices.

Coal Age. New York. Monthly.

The authoritative journal. Business and technical aspects covered, with special emphasis on operating problems.

Engineering and Mining Journal. New York. Monthly.

Cost problems and administration details, as well as over-all administration covered. Book reviews. Metal prices. Condition of industry by districts.

Iron Age. New York. Weekly.

Comprehensive coverage of a fundamental industry. Statistical features, market prices, trade progress by district, etc.

Steel. Cleveland. Weekly.

Leading periodical on its production, distribution, processing, and use. Includes current business trends, market reports, prices, statistics, and new construction.

PAPER INDUSTRY

Paper and Paper Products. New York. Semimonthly.

Manufacturing; marketing; converting. Trend of the paper industry.

Paper Trade Journal. New York. Weekly.

Covers paper production from pulp to product. Includes activities of individual mills, technical articles, market quotations.

PETROLEUM INDUSTRY

National Petroleum News. Cleveland. Weekly.

News magazine reporting trends, market developments and methods, service station planning, sales, and business conditions.

TEXTILE AND APPAREL INDUSTRY

Daily Mill Stock Reporter. New York. Daily.

Newspaper covering wool, cotton, burlap, fibers, wastes, and paper mill supplies market.

Daily News Record. New York. Daily.

Covers developments and news in textiles from raw materials through processing, merchandising, and selling.

Men's Wear. New York. Semimonthly.

Fashion trends, store locations, profitable lines, display methods. Advertising discussed in well-illustrated articles.

Textile World. New York. Monthly.

Management, merchandising, engineering, methods, materials, personnel, covered for the cotton, wool, silk, and rayon industries. Statistical and price information.

Women's Wear Daily. New York. Daily.

Gives fashion trends, developments in silk, rayon, cotton, and woolen markets for the retailer.

Directories

CHEMICAL AND DRUG INDUSTRY

Chemical Engineering Catalog and *Chemical Materials Catalog.* New York, Reinhold. Annual.

Two catalogs include sources of chemical materials and equipment listed by company, product, and trade names.

Chemical Week, Buyers Guide Issue. New York. Annual.

An up-to-date directory of both products and sources of supply. Edited specifically for buyers of raw materials, chemicals, equipment, and containers in the chemical process industries. Includes a trade name index.

Directory of Chemicals and Producers. New York, McGraw-Hill. Annual.

Contains an alphabetical listing of the various grades of chemical raw materials, fine chemicals, industrial chemicals, and dyestuffs, together with their producers and manufacturers in the United States. An alphabetical list of manufacturers and producers is also included. Pertinent shipping data.

Hayes Druggists' Directory and Commercial Reference Book. Santa Ana, Calif., Edward N. Hayes. Annual.

Retail druggists arranged by state and city with commercial and credit rating.

Oil, Paint and Drug Reporter; Green Book. New York, Schnell. Annual.

Classified list of products with manufacturers; technical, commercial, and testing services; directory of supplies.

Modern Plastics Encyclopedia. New York, Plastics Catalog Corp. Annual.

Classified list of producers of materials and chemicals, machinery and equipment, machine tools and supplies, and special services; manufacturers and molders listed by state; trade names and indexed catalog.

Rubber Red Book. New York, *Rubber Age.* Biennial.

Alphabetical, geographical, and classified lists of rubber manufacturers in the U.S. and Canada. Classified and alphabetical lists of machinery, chemicals, fabrics, rubber of all types, latex, consultants, branch offices, and trade associations.

ELECTRICAL INDUSTRY

Directory of Verified Electrical Wholesale Distributors. New York, McGraw-Hill, 1952-53.

Wholesale distributors of electric appliances and equipment in the United States and Canada. Geographic arrangement. Includes company index.

E.B.R. Electrical Buyers Reference. New York, McGraw-Hill. Annual.

A condensed catalog with descriptive advertising supplemented by classified directory of manufacturers, as well as company and trade name index.

Electronics Buyers' Guide. New York, McGraw-Hill, 1953.

Alphabetical lists of products, trade names, index of manufacturers; distributors of parts and equipment arrangement by states.

FOOD INDUSTRY

Directory of Frozen Food Processors of Fruits, Vegetables, Seafoods, Meats, etc. New York, *Quick Frozen Foods.* Annual.

Alphabetical list of frozen food processors, brand names, producers and products list, processors.

Thomas' Wholesale Grocery and Kindred Trades Register. New York, Thomas. Annual.

Geographical list of wholesale grocers in the United States, Canada, Cuba, and Puerto Rico; includes food brokers and chain stores; classified list of foods, canned goods, frozen foods, frozen food distributors, etc.

Who's Who in the Dairy Industries. New York, Urner-Barry. Annual.

Lists by state and city: butter, cheese, and ice cream manufacturers; milk processors and distributors; and cold storage warehouses. Includes federal agencies and national and state organizations; supplies and equipment dealers and chain stores.

Who's Who in the Egg and Poultry Industries. New York, Urner-Barry. Annual.

Lists by state of egg and poultry packers, processed eggs, poultry plants, cold storage warehouses; chain stores and industrial equipment, federal, state, and county officials and associations.

LEATHER INDUSTRY

Leather and Shoes Blue Book. Chicago, Rumpf. Annual.

Lists both geographically and alphabetically shoe and leather manufacturers and tanners in the United States and Canada. Also buyers, equipment, supplies, and hides. Includes associations and trade schools.

Shoe and Leather Reporter Annual. Boston. Annual.

Shoe and leather manufacturers in the United States and Canada in geographic and alphabetical lists; also dealers in materials and supplies, chains, and department stores.

METAL AND MINING INDUSTRY

Directory of Iron and Steel Works of the United States and Canada. New York, American Iron and Steel Institute. Published every three years.

List of companies, giving officers, principal products, and capacity.

Keystone Coal Buyer's Manual. New York, McGraw-Hill. Annual.

Geographic and alphabetical lists of coal sales organizations, exporting companies, coke plants, mines, and coal operators' organizations. Trade names.

Mines Register. New York, Atlas. Biennial.

Alphabetical list of active and inactive mines in the United States, Canada, and foreign countries, with history, finances, etc. Gives officials, engineers, and sources of equipment and supplies.

Standard Metal Directory. New York, Atlas. Biennial.

Geographical list of iron and steel plants in the United States and Canada, giving officers, equipment, and products. Includes foundries, metal works of all kinds, scrap dealers, export firms and brand names.

Waste Trade Directory. New York, Atlas. Biennial.

Geographical list of waste material dealers in the United States and Canada. Includes brokers, products, exporters, importers, sources of equipment, and supplies.

PAPER INDUSTRY

Lockwood's Directory of the Paper and Allied Trades. New York, Lockwood Trade Journal Co., Inc. Annual.

Geographical list of paper and pulp mills and converters in the United States, Canada, Cuba, Mexico, and South America, giving officers, capacity, etc.; classified list, mill offices, equipment and supplies, brands and watermarks.

PETROLEUM INDUSTRY

International Petroleum Register. New York. Annual.

Authoritative reference book containing information on the history, capital structure, personnel, location, and capacity of refineries and manufacturing plants, as well as production capacity, location, marketing facilities, and areas of distribution of the world's oil companies.

TEXTILE INDUSTRY

Davison's Knit Goods Trade; Rayon, Silk and Synthetic Textiles; Textile Blue Book. Ridgewood, N. J., Davison. Annual.

Geographical lists of textile mills in the United States and Canada; product lists, dealers, importers, exporters, associations.

General texts

Alderfer, E. B. and Michl, H. E., *Economics of American Industry.* New York, McGraw-Hill, 1950.

Analyzes thirty-five different industries and interprets their predominant economic characteristics. Much emphasis on recent developments. Bibliography.

Allen, E. L., *Economics of American Manufacturing.* New York, Holt, 1952.

Basic facts about major American industries and their relation to world economy.

AUTOMOTIVE INDUSTRY

Cunningham, H. M. and Sherman, W. F., *Production of Motor Vehicles*. New York, McGraw-Hill, 1951.

Intended as a guide to managerial techniques in planning, scheduling, and manufacturing motor vehicles.

CHEMICAL INDUSTRY

Haynes, William, *This Chemical Age; the Miracle of Manmade Materials*. New York, Knopf, 1942.

Studies on the historical development and present status of the chemical industries including rubber, petroleum, paper, and plastics.

Shreve, R. N., *Chemical Process Industries*. New York, McGraw-Hill, 1945.

A text on chemical engineering that stresses the relation of costs and consumption.

Snell, F. D. and Snell, C. T., *Chemicals of Commerce*. New York, Van Nostrand, 1952.

Provides information on the composition of commercial products. Includes classification of compounds by type.

FOOD INDUSTRY

Sayres, P., *Food Marketing*. New York, McGraw-Hill, 1950.

Twenty-two leaders of the food industry tell how it works. Covers marketing methods for wholesaler and retailer, the relation of the frozen food industry and the supermarket to current developments, etc.

IRON INDUSTRY

Hatcher, H. H., *Century of Iron and Men*. Indianapolis, Bobbs-Merrill, 1950.

The development of the iron mining industry in Michigan from 1845 to date.

May, E. C., *Principio to Wheeling. 1715-1945; a Pageant of Iron and Steel*. New York, Harper, 1945.

A comprehensive story of the development of a great industry. Includes a bibliography.

LEATHER INDUSTRY

Watson, M. A., *Economics of Cattlehide Leather Tannery.* Chicago, Rumpf, 1950.

A study of the production and consumption of various types of cattle-hide leather, devoting attention to the part played by labor and capital, the elements affecting marketing, and the price structure and other commercial aspects.

OIL INDUSTRY

Fanning, L. M., *Rise of American Oil.* New York, Harper, 1948.

Besides covering the development of the oil industry, it gives brief accounts of the growth of such other industries as rail and pipeline transportation, the electric industry, etc. An enlightening addition to economic history.

Fanning, L. M., *Our Oil Resources.* New York, McGraw-Hill, 1950.

Comprehensive review of economic, social, and technological developments. Covers role of private enterprise and national policy.

Schackne, S. and Duke, N. D., *Oil for the World.* New York, Harper, 1950.

A summary showing how oil can be found, drilled, transported, and used.

TEXTILE INDUSTRY

Hall, A. J., *Standard Handbook of Textiles.* London, National Trade Press, 1946.

Useful for the reader seeking a general picture of textile fibers and their manipulation.

Walton, F. L., *Tomahawks to Textiles; the Fabulous Story of Worth Street.* New York, Appleton-Century-Crofts, 1953.

The story of the development of the textile industry as reflected in its chief center.

chapter XIV

Distribution and Its Elements

Marketing and market research. Advertising and selling. Wholesale and retail trade.

Marketing and Market Research

Bibliographies

Comprehensive Marketing Bibliography, David A. Revzau, compiler. Berkeley, University of California, no date.

Carefully selected list of references arranged under twenty-one broad headings and again divided into items published before and after 1930.

Distribution Data Guide. Washington, U.S. Dept. Commerce, Office of Distribution. Monthly.

Selective list of government and nongovernment materials in the field of distribution. Besides a description of content, the source of supply is given for each item.

"Industrial Marketing as Discussed Today," *Business Literature.* Newark, N.J., Public Library, Vol. XVIII, No. 7 (March 1946).

An extensive annotated bibliography covering books, special studies, periodicals, services, directories, etc.

Marketing Research Procedure. Business Service Bulletin No. 9. Washington, U.S. Dept. Commerce, March 1954.

Annotated bibliography of materials, listed under directories, periodicals, associations, and governmental materials.

Market Research Sources. Washington, U.S. Dept. Commerce, 1950.

Improved and expanded edition of an important reference guide to sources of research literature published by private and governmental agencies. Includes studies by advertising agencies of consumer buying habits, industrial surveys by chambers of commerce, and employment data.

"Market Research Sources," *Business Literature*. Newark, N.J., Public Library, Vol. XIX, No. 6 (February 1947).

A list with detailed annotations covering selected reports and government publications.

"Marketing Studies and Consumer Analysis," *Business Literature*. Newark, N.J., Public Library, Vol. XX, No. 5 (January 1948).

A descriptive list of a number of market area studies, commodity studies, and statistics, and listing maps of trading areas as well as other special studies.

"Methods of Marketing, Distributing and Advertising in the Small Community," *Business Literature*. Newark, N.J., Public Library, Vol. XVIII, No. 3 (November 1945).

The annotated listings cover the topics under the headings consumer market and industrial market.

"Sales Engineering and Industrial Marketing," *Business Literature*. Newark, N.J., Public Library, Vol. XXV, No. 2 (October 1952).

An annotated bibliography of books and periodical references, including a list of magazines.

Selling the United States Market. Domestic Commerce Series No. 29 (New Series). Washington, U.S. Dept. Commerce, Office of Industry and Commerce, 1951.

Marketing guidebook for manufacturers and distributors, covering all aspects and including an excellent comprehensive bibliography, annotated and divided into market data, studies, and directories.

"Statistical Data for Community Appraisal," *Business Literature*. Newark, N.J., Public Library, Vol. XXIV, No. 8 (April 1952).

A list of the major publications helpful in this purpose preceded by a note on their application to particular conditions.

Annuals, handbooks, special compilations

Census of Business: Vol. I, *Retail Trade;* Vol. II, *Wholesale Trade;* Vol. III, *Service Businesses;* Vol. IV, *Construction;* Vol. V, *Distribution of Manufacturers' Sales.* Washington, U.S. Bur. Census, 1951, 1952.

This extremely detailed study of marketing provides figures on all types of establishments on a state basis, and in many cases on a larger city basis. Number of establishments, sales, number of employees, payrolls, and stock at end of year are the data supplied. The drawback to the current use of these figures is that they have not been revised since 1939.

Consumer Markets. Chicago, Standard Rate and Data Service, Inc. Annual.

Invaluable market tool containing population, sales, income, and other pertinent data for the U.S. and its subdivisions.

Economic Development Atlas. Washington, U.S. Dept. Commerce, 1950.

Shows in graphic and tabular form some of the more significant economic changes that have occurred in recent years. The changes are shown in terms of nine regions and the various states. Growth and distribution of the population, manufacturing, income, and prices are some of the topics covered.

Market Data Book, Industrial Marketing. Chicago, Advertising Publications, Inc. Annual.

Contains basic data on industrial and trade markets and the business magazines and directories serving these markets. Includes many statistical tables and data on industrial development, indicating sources for further investigation. Gives format details and total circulation. Information supplemented by descriptive advertisements.

Market Guide, Editor and Publisher. New York. Annual.

Under geographical arrangement lists American cities, giving type of community, population, locations, public service data, industries, wage earners, colleges and universities, retail and wholesale outlets, newspapers and their representatives. Same information for Canada. Includes newspaper representatives and index to surveys.

New England Community Statistical Abstracts. Boston, Bureau of Business Research, Boston University College of Business Administration, 1953.

Presents statistical, economic, and social data by states, counties, and metropolitan areas rather than by municipalities, but includes data on selected cities and towns in metropolitan areas, etc. Data cover population, area, altitudes, housing, manufacturing, distribution, payrolls, labor force, transportation, agriculture, and much other important data.

Nystrom, P. H., ed., *Marketing Handbook.* New York, Ronald, 1948.

Presents the many phases of this subject in compact and usable form. Each of the thirty sections has a detailed index. Forms and charts included.

Rand McNally Commercial Atlas and Marketing Guide. Chicago, Rand McNally. Annual.

Valuable up-to-date atlas containing a reference map for each country in the world, each state in the U.S., and each Canadian province; maps covering transportation, retail trade, population distribution, mining, and manufacturing in the U.S.; statistical and factual information about each country, and in the case of the U.S. and Canada, their subdivisions.

Sources of Regional and Local Current Business Statistics. Washington, U.S. Dept. Commerce, 1940.

Provides a ready reference list of available sources of business statistics for particular localities and regions.

State and Regional Market Indicators, 1939-1945. Washington, U.S. Dept. Commerce, 1947.

An aid in measuring the present market potential for selected market objectives.

Survey of Buying Power. New York, *Sales Management.* Annual.

Authoritative source for information on population estimates, effective buying income, and retail sales for each state by county and by municipal subdivision where available. Data on industrial potential, farm income, wholesale sales, leading cities, metropolitan areas, and Canada included.

Trading Area Marketing Maps. New York, Hearst Magazines, Marketing Division, 1952.

Each map, one for every state, is arranged according to the principal trading centers of the state and their respective consumer trading areas. Markets of first, second, and third importance are indicated by suitable legends.

Periodicals and services

Industrial Marketing. Chicago. Monthly.

Devoted to material on the problems of advertising and selling industrial products. Presents sales promotion ideas, marketing facts, case histories, industrial shows, trends, and a Washington report. *Annual Market Data and Directory* number included with subscription.

Journal of Marketing. New York, New York University, School of Retailing. Quarterly.

Articles by teachers of marketing and research experts who write from a scientific point of view. "Research in marketing, completed and in progress" summarizes research activities. Book reviews.

Directories

Bradford's Survey and Directory of Marketing Research Agencies in the United States and the World. New Rochelle, N.Y., Ernest S. Bradford, 1951.

Shows for each organization its staff and personnel, when organized, type of research, etc. Lists organizations in New York, Chicago, Philadephia, Los Angeles, Calif., Princeton, N. J., and thirty-seven other cities. Also gives marketing and research agencies in foreign countries, Dun & Bradstreet offices abroad, and membership of the World Association for Public Opinion Research.

National Roster. Evanston, Ill., American Marketing Association. Annual.

Biographical directory of members, with geographic and vocational lists.

General texts

Bradford, E. S., *Marketing Research.* New York, McGraw-Hill, 1951.

Principles and procedures for solving marketing problems, addressed primarily to college students.

Brown, L. O., *Marketing and Distribution Research.* New York, Ronald, 1949.

An understandable basic book for the business executive, clarifying the different phases, consumer surveys, distribution cost research, copy testing, situation analysis, etc.

Converse, P. D., Huegy, H. W., and Mitchell, Robert V., *The Elements of Marketing.* New York, Prentice-Hall, 1952.

One of the best texts on marketing. Comprehensive coverage of subject. Pays special attention to price controls and government regulation.

Duddy, E. A. and Revzan, David A., *Marketing; an Institutional Approach.* New York, McGraw-Hill, 1953.

"The book is designed to give a comprehensive view of what is included in 'marketing' and an understanding of the functional importance of marketing in the whole scheme of business activity."

Fox, W. M., *How to Use Market Research for Profit.* New York, Prentice-Hall, 1950.

Intended to help businessmen in general, as well as sales managers, to understand what sound market research is, and when and how to use it to produce the best results. Includes a chapter on researching of advertising media to eliminate waste and limit duplication of coverage.

Heckert, J. B. and Miner, R. B., *Distribution Costs.* New York, Ronald, 1953.

Aid to accountants and marketing executive in analysis, supervision and control of selling costs. Includes numerous charts and tables.

Lorie, J. H. and Roberts, H. L., *Basic Methods of Marketing Research.* New York, McGraw-Hill, 1951.

Contains an introduction to the subject and chapters on scientific method in "Marketing Research," "Sampling," "Communication and Observation," and "Administration of Marketing Research." Suggestions for further reading.

Luck, D. G., *Marketing Research.* New York, Prentice-Hall, 1952.

Thorough and comprehensive. The inclusion of material on copy testing, measuring audience effectiveness, and the twenty-page bibliography increase its usefulness.

Maynard, H. N. and Beckman, T. N., *Principles of Marketing*. New York, Ronald, 1946.

Excellent comprehensive text by authorities in the field. Emphasizes the ultimate consumer as well as immediate market problems and policies.

Parten, Mildred, *Surveys, Polls, and Samples*. New York, Harper, 1950.

Describes the current procedures used by population surveyors in the marketing, political opinion polling, government census, radio-audience measurements, and socioeconomic assays fields.

Payne, S. L., *The Art of Asking Questions*. Princeton, N.J., Princeton University Press, 1951.

"Treats a difficult research problem in an interesting but untechnical way." Good bibliography included.

Advertising and Selling

Bibliographies

Basic Sources in the Field of Sales and Advertising. New York, *Sales Management* (September 15, 1950).

One of the excellent bibliographies available as reprints from *Sales Management*. Covers general handbooks and directories as well as books and government publications. Lists the twenty-six "indispensables."

Books for the Advertising Man. New York, Advertising Federation of America, 1953.

Classified bibliography on advertising, marketing, and related subjects, covering publications for 1931-52. A complete and extremely useful text.

Current Reading List for Sales Executives and Salesmen. New York, *Sales Management* (March 15, 1954).

A list of selected books and bulletins of value to sales, advertising, and marketing executives.

"One Hundred Books on Advertising" (Donald H. Jones, compiler), *Journalism Series 128*, Vol. LIII, No. 17 (no date), Columbia, Mo., University of Missouri.

An annotated list divided by subject, excellent in selection and coverage.

Sources of Information for Sales Executives and Specialists, in Marketing. New York, National Sales Executives, Inc., 1954.

An aid to marketing and distribution personnel in analyzing the many functions of marketing. Included are books, periodical articles, and pamphlets on such phases as sales planning and policies, motivation and control, research, budgeting, and standardizing selling costs. It concludes with a reference shelf.

Annuals, handbooks, special compilations

Aspley, J. C., ed., *Sales Manager's Handbook.* Chicago, Dartnell, 1951.

Markets and distribution trends, practical sales research; prices and discounts; training new salesmen; compensating sales supervisors; trade promotion methods.

Aspley, J. C., ed., *The Sales Promotion Handbook.* Chicago, Dartnell, 1954.

Designed to show the use of advertising to promote sales of a new product, move merchandise after distribution, broaden the market, revive the market. Delves into the problems of organization of the department and what campaigns, techniques, media, and distribution outlets are to be considered.

Barton, Roger, ed., *Advertising Handbook.* New York, Prentice-Hall, 1950.

An attempt to cover the main aspects of advertising from consideration of the product through the problems and techniques of advertising itself to the organization of the department or agency. Glossary of technical terms is included.

Graham, Irvin, *Encyclopedia of Advertising.* New York, Fairchild, 1952.

An attempt to include all advertising terms, concepts, and usages. Examples of usage are explored and their relationships to actual practice are studied. Also included are a grouping of terms according to subject, and a directory of advertising associations.

Simmons, Harry, ed., *Sales Executives' Handbook.* New York, Prentice-Hall, 1950.

A practical handbook designed to help the executive with his planning and administration and his development of market channels. It will tell him how to build his sales organization and how to use modern marketing tools. Each section written by an executive in that field.

Periodicals and services

Advertising Age. Chicago. Weekly.

The newspaper of advertising covering current developments.

Advertising Agency and Advertising and Selling. New York. Monthly.

Covers current information on media, market, and management developments, and interprets the significant advertising trends of the day. Devoted to the needs of advertising agencies and men.

Advertising Requirements. Chicago. Monthly.

Devoted to the nonmedia features of advertising, art work, printing, premiums, prizes, radio and TV production, displays, exhibits, etc.

Dealer Relations and Sales Promotion Plans. Chicago. Dartnell.

A monthly folder of current and pertinent literature identified for filing under permanent headings: hiring salesmen, training and equipping salesmen, operating salesmen, sales meetings and conventions, sales manual material, compensating salesmen, sales contests, sales promotion, sales bulletin material, sales control, sales policy, miscellaneous.

Packaging Parade. Chicago. Monthly.

Comprehensive coverage of production, design, and materials for packaging as well as special problems. Many regular departments.

Printers' Ink. New York. Weekly.

Excellent periodical covering the advertising, selling, and marketing fields. Includes articles on the techniques and latest developments in advertising and selling. Good book reviews. Subscription includes *Advertisers Annual.*

Reporter of Direct Mail Advertising. Garden City, N.Y. Monthly.

All aspects of direct mail covered, from techniques to news and campaign planning. Case histories of successful campaigns described. Brief notes on new publications included.

Sales Management. New York. Semimonthly.

One of the outstanding magazines in its field. Includes articles on sales methods, programs, and media, as well as departments on trends, tools of selling, readers service, executive shifts, etc. The annual number, *Survey of Buying Power,* is an important book in market analysis.

Tide. New York. Fortnightly.

Presents sales and advertising trends in the various types of media. "Advertiser-Agency Trends & Forecast and Media," "Service Trends," and "Forecast" are regular departments.

Directories

McKittrick Directory of Advertisers. New York, McKittrick. Annual.

This service consists of a geographical volume listing national advertisers and the agencies handling their accounts, and an agency list giving agencies, their personnel, and their accounts, which is issued three times a year. A *Weekly Correction Service* and a *Weekly News Bulletin* are included.

Standard Advertising Register. New York, National Publishing Company. Annual.

A record of 13,000 advertisers arranged by major industry and including a trade name index. Gives officers, various department heads, and advertising agency connections. Shows advertising media used and appropriations. Forms a selective list of leading industrial firms. Supplemental publications indicate firms represented by specific advertising agencies.

General texts

Burton, P. W., Kreer, Bowman, and Gray, John B., Jr., *Advertising Copywriting*. New York, Prentice-Hall, 1949.

Good presentation of the fundamental principles of copywriting.

Caples, John, *Tested Advertising Methods*. New York, Harper, 1947.

A successful copywriter tells of advertising methods that have demonstrated their worth in practical application. Poor advertising techniques to be avoided are considered also.

Duffy, Ben, *Advertising Media and Markets*. New York, Prentice-Hall, 1951.

Discusses and analyzes the methods used in making an intelligent selection of media.

Graham, Irvin, *Advertising Campaigns.* New York, Harper, 1951.

Divided into three parts: approach to campaign planning; selection and usage of media; coordination and evaluation. Contains seven illustrated case histories.

Hobart, D. M. and Wood, J. P., *Selling Forces.* New York, Ronald, 1953.

The basic truths of selling and advertising in the United States in relation to a variety of markets.

Hotchkiss, G. B., *Outline of Advertising.* New York, Macmillan, 1950.

Excellent text, both readable and comprehensive, of the fundamentals of advertising.

Husband, R. W., *Psychology of Successful Selling.* New York, Harper, 1953.

The point of view of a professional psychologist is brought to bear on sales situations and management methods.

Kleppner, Otto, *Advertising Procedure.* New York, Prentice-Hall, 1950.

One of the top flight basic books on advertising. Includes summary of federal laws affecting advertising, a good classified bibliography, a list of information sources, and a glossary of procedure.

Maynard, H. M. and Nolen, H. C., *Sales Management,* New York, Ronald, 1950.

Good text showing how to organize for sales, plan and control sales, operate a sales force, and formulate sales policies. Contains illustrations and a bibliography.

Wholesale and Retail Trade

Bibliographies

American Business Directories. Washington, U.S. Dept. Commerce, 1947.

"Designed to help businessmen locate sources of supply and lists of prospective customers for their goods and services."

Business of Your Own, A. South Bend, Ind., Public Library, 1945.

A classified list of books and pamphlets covering the various phases of business management, as well as a list of books on how to establish your own business.

Dartnell Directory of Mailing List Sources. Chicago, Dartnell, 1948.

Useful for compiling and checking business mailing lists. Membership lists and other special types of lists are found in the volume.

"Going into Business," *Branch Library Book News.* New York, New York Public Library (May-June 1945).

A suggestive buying list of books selected for their practical application to business problems, with the emphasis on small business.

Guide to Government Information on Retailing. Washington, U.S. Dept. Commerce, Office of Domestic Commerce, 1949.

A comprehensive account of the government publications in the field, with descriptive notes.

Mail Order Business. Washington, U.S. Dept. Commerce, Inquiry Reference Service, 1949.

A bibliography of pamphlets, books, and other published materials on the subject.

"Put Your Business House in Order," *Business Literature.* Newark, N.J., Public Library, Vol. XIX, No. 9 (May 1947).

An annotated list divided under the headings "Your Own Business," "Sources of Financial Information," "Establishing Your Business," "Record Keeping," "Store Layout," "Merchandising Hints."

"Small Mail Order Business," *Business Literature.* Newark, N.J., Public Library, Vol. XXII, No. 6 (February 1950).

An annotated list of reference books, government publications, etc., on starting and operating the business, advertising the product, and sources of information.

"Why and How of a Small Business," *Business Literature.* Newark, N.J., Public Library, Vol. XVIII, No. 2 (October 1945).

An annotated bibliography on the foundation steps and management aspects of a small business. Includes many government publications.

Annuals, handbooks, special compilations

Consumers' Price Index and Retail Food Prices. Washington, U.S. Dept. Labor, Bur. Labor Statistics. Monthly.

Index numbers given for comparative dates back to 1939 for thirty-four larger cities. Average prices of certain food items in fifty-six cities noted.

Monthly Retail Trade Report, Independent Retail Stores. Washington, U.S. Dept. Commerce, Bur. Census. Monthly.

Nine regions are represented in this series, each having its monthly bulletin. Statistics are given for various businesses and by principal cities and selected counties in each region. Monthly highlights in the retail trade digested.

Monthly Wholesale Trade Report; Sales and Inventories. Washington, U.S. Dept. Commerce, Bur. Census. Monthly.

A four-page release supplying data on wholesalers' sales and inventories by kinds of business and geographic divisions. Comparative statistics are given for previous month and previous year.

Sales of Retail Chain Stores and Mail Order Houses. Washington, U.S. Dept. Commerce, Bur. Census. Monthly.

Dollar sales and index numbers are provided by kinds of business in this press release. Comparative information is found for preceding month and year.

Trends in the . . . Trade. Washington, U.S. Dept. Commerce, Bur. Census. Monthly.

Wholesale and retail sales, imports, production, etc., are given for seven selected trades: drug, dry goods, electrical goods, grocery, jewelry, tobacco, and wines and spirits.

Weekly Department Stores Sales. Washington, U.S. Board of Governors of the Federal Reserve System. Weekly.

A mimeographed sheet giving percentage changes in department store sales for the Federal Reserve districts.

Periodicals and services

Chain Store Age. New York. Monthly.

The administration edition of this periodical stresses over-all management features such as store and delivery operation, modernization, maintenance, equipment, etc.

Department Store Economist. New York. Monthly.

Comprehensive treatment covering the entire department store business. Policies in advertising, selling equipment, maintenance discussed.

Electrical Merchandising. New York. Monthly.

Emphasizes the retail end of distribution of electrical appliances and related materials.

Hardware Age. New York. Biweekly.

Basic journal for industry. Trade tips on window display, selection of lines, etc. News of personalities, new gadgets, literature, and catalogs.

Journal of Retailing. New York, New York University School of Retailing. Quarterly.

Analysis of retailing problems by members of the school's staff. Includes results of special surveys and concise book reviews.

Variety Store Merchandiser. New York. Monthly.

All aspects of management covered from merchandising, promotion, and store layout to employee training, etc.

Women's Wear Daily. New York. Daily.

General retail news and current developments in such fields as fabrics, furs, millinery, dresses, sportswear, coats, suits, etc. Section on store operations.

Directories

Chain Store Guides. New York, Chain Store Business Guide, Inc. Annuals.

These publications include *Directory of Drug Chains, Grocery and Super Market Chains, Hardware and Auto Supply Chains, 5¢-$1.00 Variety and Department Store Chains,* and *Independent 5¢-$1.00 Variety Stores.* They list stores, with addresses, buyers, and number of stores in each chain.

Directory of Automatic Merchandising. Chicago, National Automatic Merchandising Association. Annual.

Alphabetical list of manufacturers and suppliers in automatic selling; classified list of products and of vending machines and equipment.

Directory of Mailing List Houses. Washington, U.S. Dept. Commerce, Inquiry Reference Service, 1948.

Indicates those selling or renting national and regional lists of addresses. General as well as special lines covered.

Directory of the Variety Market. New York, *Variety Store Merchandiser.* Annual.

Lists manufacturers of variety store merchandise, and equipment, sales representatives, jobbers, and brand names. Geographical list of chains includes number of stores.

Hardware Age Annual Catalog and Directory Issue. Philadelphia. Annual.

Contains a catalog information index and an advertisers index as well as listings of merchandise and jobbers' brands.

Hardware Age Verified List of Hardware Wholesalers and other Related Lists. New York, *Hardware Age.* Annual.

Geographical list of wholesale houses in the United States and Canada with heavy hardware, plumbers' and tinners' supplies, manufacturers' agents, and associations.

Hayes Druggists' Directory and Commercial Reference Book. Santa Ana, Calif., Edward N. Hayes. Annual.

Retail druggists arranged by state and city, with commercial and credit rating.

Housewares Review; Directory Issue. New York, Haire. Annual.

Alphabetical listing of housewares, appliances, bathroom fittings, and garden tools, with manufacturers; also trademarks, etc.

Jewelers' Buyers Guide. New York, Sherry. Annual.

Classified list of manufacturers and importers in the jewelry industry. Includes supplies and services, associations, trade names, and trademarks. Item and company index.

Playthings Directory. New York, McCready. Annual.

Alphabetical list of toy manufacturers with addresses, products, etc. Classified list includes toys, machinery, parts, etc. Trade name list.

Sporting Goods Trade Directory. St. Louis, Mo., Spink. Annual.

Classified list of sporting goods manufacturers in the United States, alphabetical list of firms; includes trade names.

Vend Annual Market Data and Directory Almanac. Chicago, Billboard. Annual.

Vending machine manufacturers giving address, facilities, and products.

Who Makes It. New York, *Hardware Age.* Annual.

Classified list of manufacturers of hardware and allied items. Trade names.

General texts

Beckman, T. N. and Engle, N. H., *Wholesaling Principles and Practices.* New York, Ronald, 1949.

A comprehensive view with the principles, theory, and practical application of wholesaling included.

Clark, Evans, *Financing the Consumer.* New York, Harper, 1931.

All types of consumer credit agencies are analyzed from the point of view of the borrower as to costs and service. An excellent resumé of practices in the variety of finance.

Credit Sources for Small Business. Washington, U.S. Bur. Foreign and Domestic Commerce, 1945.

What should you pay for credit? How can your bank help? What are the public as well as the private sources of credit? These questions are answered for the small businessman desiring credit.

Developing and Selling New Products. Washington, U.S. Dept. Commerce, 1949.

Although written for the manufacturer, is of use to mail-order dealers trying to locate and sell the right product.

Duncan, D. J. and Phillips, C. F., *Retailing Principles and Methods.* Chicago, Irwin, 1951.

This comprehensive treatment consists of six parts: the retail field; the store and its organization; some aspects of buying and selling; operating activities and personnel; retail control; retail opportunities.

Government Financial Aids to Small Business. Washington, U.S. Bur. Foreign and Domestic Commerce, 1945.

This survey reviews the leading activities, as they relate to small business, of the Reconstruction Finance Corporation, the Federal Reserve System, the Smaller War Plants Corporation, and the Veterans Administration.

Graham, Irvin, *How to Sell Through Mail Order.* New York, McGraw-Hill, 1949.

Either the beginner or the experienced mail-order operator will find in this helpful information. Based on case histories, it discusses, in simple language, selection of products, advertising, federal regulations, and many other phases of the business.

Greenberg, D. B., *A Small Store and Independence.* New York, Greenberg, 1945.

General merchandising, displays, and financial information needed in starting a small store. Includes specific pointers on various types of stores.

Kay, E. W. and Shaw, W. F., *How to Start Your Own Business.* Chicago, Ziff-Davis, 1945.

Opportunities for successful shopkeeping and specific methods for taking advantage of them.

Keir, Alissa, *So You Want to Open a Shop.* New York, Whittlesey, 1939.

The tearoom, gift shop, beauty parlor, bookshop, flowershop, knit shop, dress shop, interior decorator, lingerie, real estate, and hat shop business receive practical attention.

Merchandise Display for Simplified Service in Department and Specialty Stores. Washington, U.S. Dept. Commerce, Office of Domestic Commerce, 1946.

Merchandise display ideas which contribute toward a greater volume of retail sales. Includes specialization of fixtures.

Record Keeping for Small Stores. Washington, U.S. Dept. of Commerce, 1942.

A manual for small retailers, describing what records are needed and how these may be kept with a minimum of time and effort.

Retail Policies; Their Selection and Application. Washington, U.S. Dept. Commerce, Office of Domestic Commerce, 1946.

Merchandise, price, promotional, and service policies are necessary, if the retail store proprietor expects to do an effective job of managing his business.

Robinson, O. P. and Haas, K. B., *How to Establish and Operate a Retail Store.* New York, Prentice-Hall, 1952.

A comprehensive treatment of the subject, which deals with financing, organizing, locating, arranging, and operating a small retail store. Emphasizes up-to-date procedures and techniques.

Selecting a Store Location. Washington, U.S. Bur. Foreign and Domestic Commerce, 1946.

Businessmen have long recognized that the right location may be an important factor in determining the success of a store. General methods of selection as well as methods practiced in selected lines are given.

Stone, R. E., *Profitable Direct Mail Methods.* New York, Prentice-Hall, 1947.

"Discusses planning of mail advertising, securing and using testimonials, selling goods by mail, and selling merchandise direct to the consumer."

Waite, W. C. and Cassady, Ralph, Jr., *Consumer and the Economic Order.* New York, McGraw-Hill, 1949.

Describes consumer problems and consumer's place in the economy.

chapter XV

The Many Aspects of Communication

Public relations and publicity. Publishing and the press. Broadcasting and television. Films in industry.

Public Relations and Publicity

Bibliographies

"Annual Reports as High Points in Interpreting Business to its Community," *Business Literature,* Newark, N.J., Public Library, Vol. XX, No. 7 (March 1948).

Annotated list of aids in their preparation, and illustrations of attention-compelling reports.

"City Government and Public Relations," *Business Literature.* Newark, N.J., Public Library, Vol. XXII, No. 5 (January 1950).

Annotated bibliography grouped by the framework for public relations, the techniques to follow, and accounts and illustrations of successful projects.

Edward L. Bernay's Collection on Public Relations. New York, Public Library, 1947.

A list of 150 volumes on the "social means of applying communications to uses in the public interest."

"Plant-Community Relations and What that Means Today," *Business Literature.* Newark, N.J., Public Library, Vol. XX, No. 10 (June 1948).

Developments in this expanding field noted, with descriptive list of references and illustrations of specific activities.

"Public Relations," *Business Information Sources.* Cleveland, Ohio, Public Library, Vol. XVIII, No. 2 (July 1947).

A lengthy annotated bibliography covering such angles as public relations in its business application, public relations as a career, etc.

"Public Relations and Business," *Business Literature.* Newark, N.J., Public Library, Vol. XXI, No. 2 (October 1948).

Annotated bibliography of materials covering developments in this field.

"Public Relations in Non-Profit Areas," *Business Literature.* Newark, N.J., Public Library, Vol. XXI, No. 3 (November 1948).

Comment on developments in this field, followed by descriptive list of pamphlets discussing techniques, and by a number of illustrations of special applications.

Public Relations, Edward L. Bernays and the American Scene. Boston, Faxon, 1951.

An annotated bibliography relating to a major figure in the field and so providing a guide to the development of public relations as a profession in the United States.

Reference Guide to the Study of Public Opinion. Princeton, N.J., Princeton University Press, 1934.

A comprehensive listing of materials dealing with the development of public opinion published prior to 1932.

Selected and Annotated Bibliography of Literature on Public Relations. Bibliography No. 3. Austin, University of Texas, Bureau of Business Research, 1948.

Annotated list grouped under general works, publics, techniques and instrumentalities, public relations counselor, public opinion, application of public relations to specific fields, and standard references.

Annuals, handbooks, special compilations

Griswold, Glen and Griswold, Denny, eds., *Your Public Relations: The Standard Public Relations Handbook.* New York, Funk & Wagnalls, 1948.

Designed as a working manual of public relations techniques. Thirty-four authorities have contributed the material based on experience in their respective fields.

Lesly, Philip, ed., *Public Relations Handbook.* New York, Prentice-Hall, 1950.

A symposium, covering the various aspects of this subject by thirty-six well-known men in the field. A bibliography and glossary are covered in the appendix.

Printers' Ink. Public Relations Idea Book. New York, Printers' Ink Publishing Company, Inc., 1953.

Tested ideas on informing employers, customers, stockholders, the public, and others, and for publicity, press notices, and house publications.

Periodicals and services

Public Relations Journal. New York, Public Relations Society of America. Monthly.

Includes articles on the methods used in publicizing activities and organizations. Studies of different communications media and activities in the field are also covered. Concise book reviews.

Public Relations News. New York, Griswold News Service. Weekly.

A four-page weekly letter with concise, stimulating comment on public relations activities, including results and incidental effects as well as original announcement. Provides a bird's-eye view on corporation thinking in its field. Guide to excellent illustrations of publications as public relations tools. Nationwide in coverage and diversified in subjects or industries discussed.

Directories

National Directory of Financial Public Relations Counsel. New York, *Financial World,* 1954-55.

Geographical list of public relations counsel exclusively in financial public relations.

Public Relations Register. New York, Public Relations Society of America, Inc., 1952.

Alphabetical list of members, gives official position, name of company, address, and type of work. Geographical and organization lists are included.

General texts

Baus, H. M., *Public Relations at Work.* New York, Harper, 1948.

Treats the elements, tools, practices, and techniques of public relations, with special emphasis on the differing publics.

Bernays, E. L., *Public Relations.* Norman, Okla., University of Oklahoma Press, 1952.

An analysis of the development of the current attitude toward public relations and case studies of its use in a variety of situations. Extensive bibliography included.

Curtis, A. P., *Is Your Publicity Showing?* Scranton, Pa., International, 1949.

A useful book written for nonprofessionals. The kinds of materials needed for different media and methods of contact are discussed.

Fine, Benjamin, *Educational Publicity.* New York, Harper, 1951.

A comprehensive discussion of public relations in the education field, that contains valuable suggestions for other applications.

Fitzgerald, S. E., *Communicating Ideas to the Public.* New York, Funk & Wagnalls, 1950.

An unusually practical and stimulating book, presenting the best techniques for opening the public's mind to a particular story.

Gallup, G. H., *Guide to Public Opinion Polls.* Princeton, N.J., Princeton University Press, 1948.

Discusses the two major sampling methods, quota and area, the question wording techniques and interview methods, qualifications of interviewers, etc.

Harlow, R. F. and Black, M. M., *Practical Public Relations.* New York, Harper, 1952.

Presents both an over-all view and an analysis of the main divisions of public relations. Discusses the tools with which it works. Suggested readings are listed at the end of many chapters.

MacDougall, C. D., *Understanding Public Opinion.* New York, Macmillan, 1952.

The why of individual and social behavior as a basis for understanding public opinion. Starting with definitions and fundamental principles, the author next examines our culture and delves into the reasons for our legends, taboos, and prejudices. He concludes with a study of the media that shape public opinion.

Sills, T. R. and Lesley, Philip, *Public Relations, Principles and Procedures.* Chicago, Irwin, 1945.

A comprehensive volume discussing molding public opinion, handling both the council and client and the future outlook.

Whyte, W. H., Jr., *Is Anybody Listening.* New York, Simon & Schuster, 1952.

Mandatory reading for executives. A study of both public and organizational communication and of the impact of the social relationship between business corporations and the executive as the family head.

Wright, J. H. and Christian, B. H., *Public Relations in Management.* New York, McGraw-Hill, 1949.

The stem to stern of public relations—employees, stockholders, customers, community government. Its every aspect has been carefully analyzed and set forth.

Publishing and the Press

Bibliographies

Book Review Digest. New York, Wilson. Annual.

Kept up to date by monthly supplements, this combines summaries of the books of the year with quotations from the reviews. Only books reviewed by the outstanding book review periodicals are covered.

Booklist; a Guide to New Books, The. Chicago, American Library Association. Semimonthly.

A descriptive list of new books arranged by subject, intended primarily as an aid to selection for smaller libraries.

"Business Book Information Sources," *Business Literature.* Newark, N.J., Public Library, Vol. XXII, No. 8-9 (April-May 1950).

Descriptive list of periodicals regularly carrying business book reviews in specialized as well as general fields.

Business Information Sources, Business Information Bureau. Cleveland, Ohio, Public Library. Irregular.

A list of books, with annotations, supplemented by magazine articles. Each issue is devoted to one main subject with subdivisions.

Business Literature. Newark, N.J., Public Library. Monthly, September-June.

A bibliographical treatment of current business questions, published since 1928. Includes annotated lists by subject of many business books, periodicals, and other publications and discussions of their uses and development.

"Business Periodicals for the Small Public Library," *Business Literature.* Newark, N.J., Public Library, Vol. XXVII, No. 3 (November-December 1954).

A descriptive list grouped by subject of the major business periodicals in the fields of widest interest.

"House Organs as Company Interpreters," *Business Literature.* Newark, N.J., Public Library, Vol. XXI, No. 9 (May 1949).

Descriptive list of books, pamphlets, and magazine articles on the production of house organs. Includes a short list of notable periodicals of this type.

Industrial Arts Index. New York, Wilson.

A monthly index to the articles in over 200 periodicals in the fields of business, finance, science, and technology. Cumulated at intervals. Available in many libraries.

New York Times Index. New York. Bimonthly and annual.

Subject index to this newspaper, both daily and Sunday issues. References indicate page, column, and date, with selected section numbers added for Sunday issues. Brief summary is invaluable in locating dates of events and happenings, serving as a guide to articles in other publications. Annual number contains "outstanding events of the year" in chronological order.

Public Affairs Information Service Bulletin. New York, Public Affairs Information Service. Weekly.

A weekly index to current books, pamphlets, periodical articles, government documents, and other material in the field of economics and public affairs. Emphasis is on factual and statistical information. Cumulated five times a year.

Publishers Trade List Annual. New York, Bowker. Annual.

A trade bibliography consisting of individual publishers' catalogs bound together.

Reader's Guide to Periodical Literature. New York, Wilson. Semimonthly.

An index to the some hundred odd magazines most often used in general reference work. Cumulated at intervals. Available in most libraries. Covers limited number of business magazines.

Technical Book Review Index. New York, Special Libraries Association. Monthly.

Digests of book reviews of scientific, technical, and business books are published without comment. Too specialized to carry many reviews of general business books.

United States Catalog. New York. Wilson.

A series of volumes listing books in print, noting publisher, price, etc. The basic record kept to date by the monthly publication of the *Cumulative Book Index* cumulated at irregular intervals during the year and into an annual volume.

Annuals, handbooks, special compilations

Market Data Book Number, Industrial Marketing. Chicago, Advertising Publications, Inc. Annual.

Contains basic data on industrial and trade markets and the business papers serving these markets. Gives format details and total circulation, supplemented by descriptive advertisements for many periodicals; many giving detailed information on editorial scope, data on editorial staff, etc.

Publisher's Weekly, Annual Trade Statistics. New York. Annual.

A review of the year for the publishing industry that discusses not only production but trends and problems. Includes analysis of output.

Periodicals and services

Editor and Publisher. New York. Weekly.

Comprehensive coverage of newspaper field, including news gathering, management, and publishing problems.

Publishers' Weekly. New York. Weekly.

Includes articles on book publishing and book marketing and carries comprehensive listing of books as they are published. The basic information source for this data.

Retail Bookseller. Hillside, N.J. Monthly.

Special emphasis placed on book merchandising, rental libraries. News of current publications.

Writer. Boston. Monthly.

The writer's adviser on all aspects of freelance writing. Extensive market news section.

Directories

Directory of Newspapers and Periodicals. Philadelphia, Ayer. Annual.

A guide to publications printed in the United States and its possessions, listing them geographically and noting publication date, general characteristic, editor, etc. Classified lists of agricultural, general, trade, technical, and class publications, grouped by subject are included.

Editorial Directory. New York, Galub, 1953.

Lists business, industrial, and professional publications under interest groups. Alphabetical index. Descriptive note includes editorial personnel, editorial content and features, payment policy, and types of readers.

International Yearbook. New York, *Editor & Publisher.* Annual.

A comprehensive listing of newspapers and newspaper personnel, together with information on related groups such as the news services.

Nation's Leading House Magazines. New York, Gebbie. Annual.

Alphabetical company list of house magazines giving title, editor, circulation, type of readers, etc.; also title and geographical lists.

Newspaper Rates and Data. Evanston, Ill., Standard Rate and Data Service. Annual.

Advertising rates, etc., in business publications, consumer magazines, newspapers, radio, and television in the United States.

Printers' Ink Directory of House Organs; Internal—External—Combination. New York, Printers' Ink Publishing Company, 1950.

Contains a comprehensive editorial checklist section on house organ editing and publishing, followed by an alphabetical list of house organ titles, an alphabetical list of sponsors, and a geographical list of sponsors.

Ulrich's Periodicals Directory. New York, Bowker, 1947.

A classified guide to a selected list of current foreign and domestic periodicals. As the approximate number of entries is 7500, it serves as the key to many sources not generally noted. About sixty-five business subject classifications are included.

Working Press of the Nation. Burlington, Iowa, National Research Bureau, Inc., 1955.

A directory covering all angles of the newspaper world. Features include personnel of newspapers in cities over 50,000, feature writers by subject, news services, etc.

Writer's Market. Cincinnati, Ohio, *Writer's Digest,* 1952.

Lists writers' markets in magazines in every field. Also photographic market and agencies, syndicates, and writer's clubs. Gives type of material acceptable and rates of pay.

General texts

Bently, Garth, *Editing the Company Publication.* New York, Harper, 1953.

Covers publications prepared for consumers and distributors as well as employees.

Elfenbein, Julien, *Business Journalism, Its Function and Future.* New York, Harper, 1947.

A comprehensive study enlightening to general readers as well as to those associated with the industry. Covers the development and present status of the trade press and the function of those responsible for its activities. Includes chronological list of American business papers before 1900.

Elfenbein, Julien, *Businesspaper Publishing Practice.* New York, Harper, 1952.

Deals with accounting, circulation, advertising, sales promotion, and production phases of administration as well as with the problems touching the editorial department and the question of public responsibility.

Herzberg, J. G., *Late City Edition.* New York, Holt, 1947.

An account by a newspaper editor and his associates of all the aspects of the production of a metropolitan daily from the basic news gathering to the mechanics of its final coordination.

Svirsky, Leon, ed., *Your Newspaper: Blueprint for a Better Press.* New York, Macmillan, 1947.

A systematic analysis and criticism of modern newspapers made by a group of Nieman Fellows, resulting in a program for a model newspaper from layout and contents to staff requirements and financing.

Warren, C. M., *Modern News Reporting.* New York, Harper, 1951.

An over-all account of all the elements valuable in indicating points to be taken into consideration in the release of news.

Woolf, D. G., *Business Paper Editor at Work.* New York, McGraw-Hill, 1936.

Concise but stimulating record of the many ways in which the editing of business papers is involved with the many ramifications of industry.

Broadcasting and Television

Bibliographies

Radio and Television Bibliography, Bulletin 1948 No. 17. Washington, U.S. Federal Security Agency, Office of Education, 1948.

A comprehensive, annotated list covering all phases from equipment and programs to careers.

Rose, Oscar, *Radio Broadcasting and Television.* New York, Wilson, 1947.

An exceptionally comprehensive and well-annotated bibliography covering all aspects of broadcasting. Television is covered to the extent possible at date of publication.

"Television in Business and Industry," *Business Information Sources.* Cleveland, Ohio, Public Library, Vol. XX, No. 2 (September 1949).

An annotated and comprehensive bibliography showing the business applications as of that date.

Annuals, handbooks, special compilations

Hodapp, William, *Television Manual.* New York, Farrar, Straus, and Young, 1953.

Guide to TV production and programming for education, public affairs, and entertainment.

Television Factbook. Washington Radio News Bureau. Semiannual.

Comprehensive handbook giving statistics of advertising, directors of television stations, personnel, etc.

UNESCO, Television. A World Survey. New York, Columbia University Press, 1953.

Lists television facilities, programs, sources of revenue for stations established early in 1953, and plans for the future in each of forty-five countries and the United Nations.

Periodicals

Broadcasting-Telecasting. Washington. Weekly.

Current news on all phases of industry given wide coverage.

Motion Picture Daily. New York. Daily.

Gives complete news of the motion picture trade and covers developments in radio and television.

Radio-Television Daily. New York. Daily.

Covers radio and television development, including government rulings, station news, etc.

Directories

Broadcasting Yearbook. Washington, Broadcasting Publications, Inc. Annual.

Radio stations in the United States, Canada, and Latin America, arranged by location, call letters, and frequencies; national and regional networks; program services; equipment manufacturers; FCC rules; advertising agencies and clients; and associations.

Motion Picture and Television Almanac. New York, Quigley. Annual.

Life sketches of people in the motion picture industry; includes corporations, theater circuits, film lists, awards, organizations. Similar data on television.

General texts

Allen, Fred, *Treadmill to Oblivion.* Boston, Little, Brown, 1954.

A witty, sharply delineated record of the life and death of an outstanding radio program, caustically illustrating the pitfalls of that aspect of the industry.

Chester, Giraud and Garrison, Granet, *Radio and Television.* New York, Appleton, 1950.

An excellent general introduction to all aspects including the impact as a social force. Bibliography.

Evans, J. A., *Selling and Promoting Radio and Television.* New York, *Printers' Ink,* 1954.

Comprehensive study of the different elements of radio and television broadcasting, including such supplementary aids as research services and market and media information.

Hutchinson, T. H., *Here is Television; Your Window to the World.* New York, Hastings, 1947.

A nontechnical discussion of the whole picture of television production from the first steps to the finished production and its impact. The principal emphasis is on program and production.

Settel, Irving and Glenn, Norman, *Television, Advertising and Production Handbook.* New York, Crowell, 1953.

A group of experts treats all phases of the commercial aspects of television programs and production, including selling, promotion, financing, and research.

Wolfe, C. H., *Modern Radio Advertising.* New York, Funk & Wagnalls, 1953.

How to get better advertising results from air-wave activity via national networks, spot broadcasting, and in relation to local stations.

Films in Industry

Bibliographies

"Business Film and Its Function," *Business Literature*. Newark, N.J., Public Library, Vol. XXII, No. 7 (March 1950).

Annotated bibliography of books on the development of industrial films, sources of supply, and film use in industry and advertising.

Educational Film Guide. New York, Wilson. 1953.

Both an alphabetic title and subject list of 7030 films and a selected, classified, and annotated list of 4190 films. The indexing makes this an indispensable tool.

Annuals, handbooks, special compilations

Curran, C. W., *Handbook of TV and Film Techniques*. New York, Pellegrini, 1953.

Covers motion picture and TV film production, and production costs for both. Special emphasis on business use of media. Includes glossary of motion picture nomenclature.

Index of Training Films. Chicago, *Business Screen*. Annual.

A comprehensive listing of more than 2000 industrial motion pictures and slidefilms and their sources, for reference and training use in industry and vocational education.

Periodicals

Business Screen. Chicago. Monthly.

Valuable for its case histories of film programs in large corporations and its guide to current available films, as well as for news of the industry.

Film World & A-V World. Los Angeles. Monthly.

All aspects of the audio-visual industry, use and production of 16 mm motion pictures, new equipments, etc.

Directories

Educator's Guide to Free Films. Randolph, Wis., Educator's Progress Service. Annual.

Good material on the sources of supply, by one of the pioneers in the field.

Membership List and Trade Directory. Evanston, Ill., National Audio-Visual Association. Annual.

A geographical listing of the 453 member dealers. Key numbers indicate the types of service and materials each member offers.

General texts

Gipson, H. C., *Films in Business and Industry.* New York, McGraw-Hill, 1947.

Authoritative presentation of the value and use of films, pointing out common errors made in the past. Technical factors, cost, and distribution are explained. Appendix includes handy trade information.

Haas, K. B. and Packer, Henry, *Preparation and Use of Visual Aids.* New York, Prentice-Hall, 1946.

Each chapter includes a brief, practical presentation of a visual aid. Well adapted to industrial training.

New Horizons for Business Films. New York, Films Committee, Association of National Advertisers, 1947.

The days of the heavy-handed commercial film may soon be over; for the business film is a tool to be handled with deftness, not swung like a bludgeon.

Waldron, Gloria, *The Information Film. A Report of the Public Library Inquiry.* New York, Columbia University Press, 1949.

This book examines the entire field of the adult education film. The problems of distribution and library use are stressed. Bibliography of books, periodicals, and catalogs.

chapter XVI

Information and the Individual

Moving up the ladder. Personal economics and information needs. Retirement—the door to a new career.

Moving Up the Ladder

Bibliographies

"Executive Development," *Business Information Sources.* Cleveland, Ohio, Public Library, Vol. XXIII, No. 3 (July-September 1952).

An extensive annotated bibliography covering all phases of self-development and company selection and training.

"Executives Wanted," *Business Literature.* Newark, N.J., Public Library, Vol. XXVII, No. 8 (April 1955).

An annotated bibliography of helps to a successful business career through self-development.

"Opportunity and Women Today," *Business Literature.* Newark, N.J., Public Library, Part I, Vol. XXV, No. 1 (September 1952); Part II, Vol. XXV, No. 7 (March 1953).

A descriptive bibliography of materials on opportunities in accounting, advertising, banking, food trade, journalism, medicine, public service, science, etc.

General texts

Arthur, J. K., *Jobs for Women over Thirty-Five.* New York, Prentice-Hall, 1947.

It isn't easy for the fortyish female to land a job, but this practical book gives shrewd advice on how to hurdle the barriers of age and sex. Includes documented statistics, case histories, a bibliography, and sources of help you should know.

Brophy, Loire, *There's Plenty of Room at the Top.* New York, Simon & Schuster, 1946.

How to attain business success and how to get along with people in business. Much intelligent and stimulating comment based on the author's experience as an advisor for business firms.

Hegarty, E. J., *Showmanship in Public Speaking.* New York, McGraw-Hill, 1952.

A practical guide, based on the author's thirty years experience. Advice on testing material for its interest, how to handle notes, overcoming nervousness, and keeping listeners alert are among the topics discussed.

MacGibbon, E. G., *Fitting Yourself for Business.* New York, McGraw-Hill, 1947.

Furnishes a sound basis for personality development, and at the same time acquaints the student with what an employer expects of the novice in business. Down-to-earth and detailed but vivid in the illustrations discussed. Topics range from technical efficiency to details of personal appearance—all treated with candor and clarity.

Mead, Shepherd, *How to Succeed in Business Without Really Trying.* New York, Simon & Schuster, 1952.

A compact handy guide written in humorous vein, but filled with useful information on how to succeed. Some of the topics covered are how to dispose of rivals, how to leave meetings, etc.

Miles, L. F., *Brass Hat or Executive.* New York, Wilfred Funk, 1949.

A stimulating and outspoken guide to appropriate and progressive conduct in the successful search for advancement.

Moore, R. E., *How Am I Doing?* New York, Forbes, 1952.

A practical book for executives to help them plan their own executive development program. Self-analysis charts and blueprints are included. There is also helpful information for those changing their jobs, on procedures, resumés, and interviews.

Reilly, W. J., *How to Avoid Work.* New York, Harper, 1949.

Fresh, crisp advice on picking the right job for yourself, which, when done, ceases to be work.

Starch, Daniel, *How to Develop Your Executive Ability.* New York, Harper, 1943.

Based on an analysis of the business careers of 150 present-day executives, including top, middle, and lower-level concerns. How executives organize their thinking, how they tackle their work, how they handle people, how they fit themselves for responsibility, the four factors necessary for development of executive talent are stressed.

Uris, Auren, *How to Become a Successful Leader.* New York, McGraw-Hill, 1953.

Discusses the business, educational, and social problems that must be solved, and presents a program for their solution.

Wilson, E. B., *Getting Along with People in Business.* New York, Funk & Wagnalls, 1950.

A basic guide giving detailed information on how to get along with supervisors, associates, and subordinates in business. Well organized and illustrated with examples.

Witty, Paul, *How to Become a Better Reader.* Chicago, Science Research Associates, 1953.

Shows how and why improved reading skills are necessary today, and gives twenty lessons toward this end.

Personal Economics and Information Needs

Bibliographies

"Everyday Economics," *Business Literature.* Newark, N.J., Public Library, Vol. XXIV, No. 1 (September 1951).

Descriptive list of references helpful to the individual.

"Life Insurance and Personal Economics," *Business Literature.* Newark, N.J., Public Library, Vol. XXVI, No. 3 (November 1953).

An annotated bibliography including references on the points to be considered by the investor in life insurance.

"Managing Your Pocketbook," *Business Literature.* Newark, N.J., Public Library, Vol. XXVI, No. 7 (March 1954).

An annotated list of references on the business detail of living, including current management, planning for the future, the question of home ownership, etc.

"Where to Work and Live," *Business Literature.* Newark, N.J., Public Library, Vol. XVIII, No. 1 (September 1945).

Selective annotated list of information sources on the various factors to be considered in making a community analysis or selecting a home.

Annuals, handbooks, special compilations

Survey of Buying Power. New York, *Sales Management.* Annual.

Authoritative source for information on population estimates, effective buying income, and retail sales for each state, by county and by municipal subdivision where available. Data on industrial potential, farm income, wholesale sales, leading cities, metropolitan areas, and Canada included. Useful as guide to standard of living in communities covered.

Periodicals and services

Changing Times. Washington. Monthly.

General business reading, widely diversified in subject and geared to the range of interest and experience of the average business reader. Fills the long vacant place of a magazine for all-around reading from the individual's business angle. Treats municipal well-being, possible depressions, developments in an industry, personal problems in their relation to economic welfare and on a scale that relates them to individual responsibilities.

Housing Letter. New York, Housing Institute. Fortnightly.

A fortnightly interpretive news digest of housing trends and opportunities. Simple and clear in style and keyed to small broker, landlord, and tenant experience rather than to broad economic phases.

Directories

American Library Directory. New York, Bowker. Triennial.

Classified list of 11,920 public, educational, and special libraries in the United States and Canada, arranged geographically, giving statistical data and directing personnel.

American Medical Directory. Chicago, American Medical Association, 1950.

Lists physicians in the U.S. and Canada, with professional information. Includes lists of hospitals, medical societies, colleges giving degrees in medicine, etc.

Living Church Annual; the Yearbook of the Episcopal Church. New York, Morehouse-Gorham. Annual.

Primarily a directory of the diocesan and parochial lists and the institutions and organizations of the church in the United States. Includes statistical and other special data.

Patterson's American Educational Directory. Wilmette, Ill., Educational Directories, Inc. Annual.

Useful reference tool including a geographical section, a classified section, a library directory, an alphabetical list of schools, college, and university colors, educational associations, and an educational business directory.

Polk's Bankers Encyclopedia. Detroit, Polk. Annual.

A complete bank directory arranged by state and giving officers, resources, liabilities, and principal correspondents. Includes information on state officials and regulations as well as lists of investment dealers, directory of legal reserve life insurance companies, and much related material.

Poor's Register of Directors and Executives, United States and Canada. New York, Standard & Poor's. Annual.

A national directory of leaders in finance and industry, covering some 90,000 names, giving both the associations of individuals and the geographic distribution data on 18,000 corporations, and listing directors, officers, some department heads, and accountants.

Who's Who in America. Chicago, Marquis. Biennial.

Biographical sketches and addresses of 33,893 notable Americans. Geographically indexed.

General texts

Bigelow, H. F., *Family Finance.* Philadelphia, Lippincott, 1953.

Designed to help the average family solve financial problems by presenting basic information for long-range planning. Topics include financing an automobile, the housing problem, college educations, vacations, planning a good food budget, etc.

Bowe, W. J., *Tax Planning for Estates.* Nashville, Tenn., Vanderbilt University Press, 1949.

The wise, who wish to leave their affairs in order for their heirs, will study this book, with its solutions to the many problems of wills and estate planning too often left unfaced.

Finke, M. B. and Knoh, Helen, *Moneywise.* New York, Putnam, 1950.

Written by two women, each with twenty years of experience as manager of the women's department of a famous bank. It provides intelligent women who have money to manage with essential information about handling it. How to open a checking account, using consumer credit, taxes, social security, etc. discussed.

Johnston, K. B., *Building or Buying a House.* New York, McGraw-Hill, 1945.

Practical suggestions and warnings about the many problems related to home ownership. Discusses selecting the site, financing, agreements and contracts, judging house construction, etc.

Jones, S. V., *How to Get it From the Government.* New York, Dutton, 1951.

Uncle Sam offers something to everybody. This concise handbook explains the principal benefits every citizen is entitled to receive from the federal government, including social security and old age pension, veterans' benefits, home, farm, and business loans, and use of public lands.

Jordan, D. F., *On Investments.* New York, Prentice-Hall, 1941.

Written from the point of view of the man who manages his own investments. One of the most useful books in its field. Includes chapters on sources of information and also how to read the financial page.

Lasser, J. K. and Porter, S. F., *Managing Your Money.* New York, Holt, 1953.

A valuable blueprint "packed with facts for planning one's financial progress." Includes chapters on the social security program and how to get the most out of it.

Lasser, J. K., *Your Income Tax.* New York, Simon & Schuster, 1953. Annual.

This annual tax guide, written for the layman, shows how to prepare personal income tax returns. Includes many tables.

Merrill, Lynch, Pierce, Fenner and Beane, *How to Read a Financial Report.* New York, 1947.

A clearly illustrated interpretation of the divisions of a financial statement which must be understood for wise investment.

Morgan, A. B., *Investors' Road Map.* Author, Box 10, Bristol, R.I., 1953.

An informal and practical treatment of the problems met by the inexperienced investor. A highly personalized and lively little book by a woman who conducts investment classes as a community service and who, in readable style, conveys a more than rudimentary knowledge of investments.

Radell, N. H., *Accounting for the Individual and Family.* New York, Prentice-Hall, 1940.

Presents in a nontechnical way, a system of keeping records which can be made as simple as desired. It indicates also patterns of economic living as standards in relation to income and spending.

Rogers, D. I., *Teach Your Wife to be a Widow.* New York, Holt, 1953.

Contains information helpful to widows and to married men helping their wives develop an understanding of financial management.

Rostenberg, Walter, *House for Sale.* New York, Stravon, 1952.

Designed as a practical guide to the layman who has property for sale. Discusses such topics as setting the price, initiating the sale, listing with brokers, legal matters, mortgages, do's and don'ts, and other miscellaneous information.

RETIREMENT—THE DOOR TO A NEW CAREER

Bibliographies

Classified Bibliography on Geriatrics and the Care of the Aged. J. J. Griffin, 57 School St., Somerville, Mass., 1950.

Contains about 1200 titles of general and specialized literature on this subject.

Employment and Retirement in an Aging Population: A Bibliography. Boston, Harvard University, Graduate School of Business Administration, Baker Library, 1951.

Literature covering job performance, employment, retirement, and background material. An annotated list of bibliographies is included.

"Looking Ahead," *Harvard Business Review.* Boston, July-August, 1952.

Survey and bibliography of geriatrics literature.

"Pensions—Important to All," *Business Literature.* Newark, N.J., Public Library, Vol. XXIV, No. 2 (October 1951).

An annotated bibliography of references to materials on the problems involved in establishing a pension system.

Preparing Employees for Retirement. Princeton, N.J., Princeton University, Industrial Relations Section, May 1951.

An annotated bibliography on the economic, social, and psychological problems of aged workers.

"Retirement: Preparation, Timing, Implications," *Business Information Sources.* Cleveland, Ohio, Public Library, Vol. XXIII, No. 2 (March-June 1952).

Annotated bibliography on the changing concepts of retirement and the recognition given them as factors in business development.

Selected Bibliography on Employment of the Older Worker, C. C. Gibbons, compiler. Kalamazoo, Mich., W. E. Upjohn Institute for Community Research, 1951.

Reports, pamphlets, and magazine articles.

Selected List of References on Aging. Washington, U.S. Federal Security Agency, 1950.

Social, economic, and medical aspects of an aging population.

Selected References on Aging. Washington, U.S. Federal Security Agency, 1952.

An annotated bibliography listing literature on the social, economic, and medical aspects of aging. Includes general references and conference reports, conference and group discussion methods, and bibliographies.

"Some Economic Aspects of Retirement," *Business Literature.* Newark, N.J., Public Library, Vol. XXVII, No. 5 (January 1955).

An annotated bibliography covering the effect of the changes in the tax law, the importance of variable annuities, the application of the social security amendments, and methods by which retirement can be profitable.

Timing Retirement. Princeton, N.J., Princeton University, Industrial Relations Section, January 1952.

An annotated list.

"'Your Second Career,' How to Find the Doors Retirement Opens," *Business Literature.* Newark, N.J., Part I, Vol. XXIII, No. 9 (May 1951); Part II, Vol. XXV, No. 8 (April 1953).

Comprehensive descriptive list of books, pamphlets, and magazine articles on the various approaches to the changes in living practices brought by retirement. Includes material on company programs as well as individual planning.

General texts

Baird, Janet H., *These Harvest Years.* New York, Doubleday, 1951.

What do each of us want in the years which come after forty? This book sets forth a blueprint for laying the foundation now for maintenance of health, spiritual values, and economic security. Written by specialists who discuss occupations for retirement, travel, the community's part in the picture, etc.

Blanchard, F. S., *Where to Retire and How.* New York, Dodd, Mead, 1952.

A highly selective picture of seventy-five good retirement spots. The book is aimed at the $3000-$10,000 income after retirement group. A guide to jobs, hobbies, housing, planning, cost of living, climates, and places.

Boynton, P. W., *Six Ways to Retire.* New York, Harper, 1952.

Practical ideas on how to make retirement a rewarding experience. Points out how to choose a place to live, how to discover hidden talents, and how to pay your way.

Buckley, J. C., *Retirement Handbook.* New York, Harper, 1953.

Practical guide in planning and preparing for retirement. Discusses income planning, selecting a place to live, and operating a small business. Includes a retirement planning schedule, a table of climatic data for selected cities in the United States, and a chart showing the cost of living in selected localities.

Ford, N. D., *Where to Retire on a Small Income.* New York, Harian, 1951.

Where shall I live upon retiring? This booklet presents a brief but critical analysis of various geographical regions of the United States, pointing out advantages and disadvantages of each.

Giles, Ray, *Begin Now—To Enjoy Tomorrow.* Newark, N.J., Mutual Benefit Life Insurance Company, 1951.

Stimulating, constructive, and full of sound common sense in its emphasis on the steps to take today so that the act of retirement is a step in enjoyable living, not a stop at a dead end.

Giles, Ray, *How to Retire—and Enjoy It.* New York, McGraw-Hill, 1949.

Sound advice on planning for retirement by saving toward economic security and by developing hobbies for leisure time. Suggests such forms of savings as insurance and investments, and discusses many hobbies, some financially profitable.

Johnson, W. M., *The Years After Fifty.* New York, McGraw-Hill, 1947.

Sums up for those who have reached the halfway mark a useful and practical philosophy of living. Written by a practicing physician, it discusses the various problems, physical, mental, and spiritual, peculiar to this period. Sound medical advice is given in simple language. Includes a bibliography.

Lawton, George, *Aging Successfully*. New York, Columbia University Press, 1946.

Recommended to readers over forty "who can take plain talk" and benefit from it. Discusses the problems of men who have worked hard all their lives, so that they can retire in their old age, but who have failed to realize the necessity for planning what to do when their present job is past.

Lehman, Maxwell and Yarmon, Morton, *Jobs After Retirement*. New York, Holt, 1954.

Describes many full and part-time jobs and illustrates them with case histories. Gives advice on how to find work, and lists thirteen cities in which the "Forty Plus Club" operates. Lists "suitable occupations" for men over 50 and home industries. An excellent guide.

Stieglitz, E. J., *The Second Forty Years*. Philadelphia, Pa., Lippincott, 1946.

A clear and excellent discussion of the problems of aging, written by a practicing physician. Gives advice on achieving health and happiness over and after forty. Wise use of leisure is one of the phases discussed.

chapter XVII

Guides to Information Sources

Statistical data. Business information guides. Government publications. Indexes. Maps, atlases, and gazetteers.

Statistical Data

Annuals, handbooks, special compilations

Agricultural Finance Review. Washington, U.S. Bur. Agricultural Economics. Annual with supplements.

Valuable data on farm credit, farm insurance, and farm taxation. Comment and statistics.

Agricultural Statistics. Washington, U.S. Dept. Agriculture. Annual.

Brings together the more important series of statistics compiled in this department and others whose work concerns agriculture.

Banking and Monetary Statistics. Washington, Board of Governors of the Federal Reserve System, 1943.

Makes available in one place and on a uniform basis statistics on banking, monetary, and other financial developments for, with some exceptions, the period 1914 to December, 1941.

County and City Data Book. Washington, U.S. Bur. Census. Annual.

Designed to meet the need for statistics for small geographic areas. Collects data scattered in a number of publications or obtainable by inquiries to specific governmental or private agencies.

Dewhurst, Frederick and Associates, *America's Needs and Resources.* New York, Twentieth Century Fund, 1955.

A comprehensive inventory of our economic resources and productive capacity. It is a measure of this nation's activities, achievements, and prospects.

Economic Almanac. New York, National Industrial Conference Board. Annual.

Statistics and information not found in the *Statistical Abstract* are often included in this publication. In some instances data are more up to date. Contains alphabetical designation of government agencies and "Glossary of Selected Terms" defining those in current use. Indexed.

Handbook of Basic Economic Statistics. Washington, Economic Statistics Bur. Monthly.

A compact, up-to-date source of more than 1500 authentic, government-compiled basic statistical series covering most aspects of the national economy. Includes a monthly summary of national business conditions and economic highlights.

Handbook of Labor Statistics. Washington, U.S. Bur. Labor Statistics, 1950.

Invaluable guide to industry starting in 1926. All the major statistical series compiled by the Bureau are included. Sections include prices and cost of living; earnings, hours, and wage rates, etc.

Historical Statistics of the United States, 1789-1945; a Supplement to the Statistical Abstract. Washington, U.S. Bur. Census, 1949. Continuation to 1952, Washington, 1954.

Historical statistics that portray the status of U.S. in various fields at various times. Valuable as they are limited in accessibility and compilation.

Statistical Abstract of the United States. Washington, U.S. Bur. Census. Annual.

An accumulation of statistics on American activities and development covering a long period of years. Covers populations, vital statistics, immigrations, finance, railroads, commerce, etc. Contains a list of government bibliographies. Fully indexed.

Survey of Current Business, Annual Review Number. Washington, Government Printing Office.

An analysis of the previous year's business highlights. Discusses national income and product, production and trade, and foreign transactions.

United Nations Statistical Yearbook. New York, United Nations. Annual.

Worldwide statistical tables covering population, manpower, agriculture, manufacturing, etc. Subject and country indexes facilitate use.

Periodicals and services

Dun's Statistical Review. New York. Monthly.

Camposed wholly of statistical tables, it presents the latest data on bank clearings, business failures, price indices, building permit values, and new business incorporations. Includes a group of economy indicators.

Federal Reserve Bulletin. Washington. Monthly.

Summary of business conditions, supplemented by financial industrial and commercial statistics of U.S. and foreign countries. Federal Reserve statistics by districts. Board's official means of communication with member banks.

Journal of the American Statistical Association. Chicago. Quarterly.

A scholarly periodical devoted to articles on statistical theory and method. Includes abstracts of articles and book reviews.

Monthly Bulletin of Statistics. New York, United Nations. Monthly.

World economic statistics by country. Covers population, manpower, forestry, industrial production, mining, transportation, internal and external trade, wages and prices, national income, and finance.

Monthly Labor Review. Washington, U.S. Dept. Labor. Monthly.

Important statistical information on fluctuation in the cost of living, wages and hours of labor, wholesale and retail prices, etc. Book reviews.

Statistical Bulletin. Washington, U.S. Securities and Exchange Commission. Monthly.

Contains such regular monthly series as new securities offerings for cash, sales on securities exchange, common stock price indexes, round lot and odd lot transactions on New York exchanges. Quarterly are other statistics on securities as well as on individual saving and corporation finance.

Survey of Current Business. Washington. Monthly.

The major reporting publication for business statistics, including indexes for income payments, industrial production, commodity prices, statistics on construction and real estate, domestic trade, employment conditions and wages, finance, foreign trade, transportation and communication, products by kind, etc. Some reports on the business situation and conditions in specific industries are included.

Treasury Bulletin. Washington. Monthly.

This official organ of the Treasury Department consists entirely of statistical tables and charts on all phases of public finance.

Business Information Guides

Bibliographies

American Business Directories, Industrial Series No. 67. Washington, U.S. Dept. Commerce, 1947.

Classified list of directories for business and industry, giving address, price, and coverage. Gives regional directories for industry when issued. Includes separate list of industrial directories by state.

"Business Aids for the Reference Collection," *Business Literature.* Newark, N.J., Public Library, Vol. XXVI, No. 10 (June 1954).

Annotated bibliography of some sixty basic business information sources, including bibliographies, handbooks, directories, etc.

"Business Book Information Sources," *Business Literature.* Newark, N.J., Public Library, Vol. XXII, Nos. 8, 9 (April, May 1950).

Descriptive list of periodicals regularly carrying business book reviews in specialized as well as general fields.

"Business Periodicals for the Small Public Library," *Business Literature.* Newark, N.J., Public Library, Vol. XXVII, No. 3 (November-December 1954).

A descriptive list grouped by subject of the major business periodicals in the fields of widest interest.

Clark, D. T. and Goldsby, Margaret, *Selected List of Annual "Statistical" and "Review" Issues of American Business Periodicals (Reference List 9).* Boston, Harvard University, Baker Library, 1951.

"Selected Business Directories," *Business Literature.* Newark, N.J., Public Library, Vol. XXVI, Nos. 4-6 (December 1953, January 1954, and February 1954).

Part I deals with directories with general coverage; Parts II and III with specialized directories. An annotated list giving publisher, date, and frequency.

"State Industrial Directories," *Business Literature.* Newark, N.J., Public Library, Vol. XXIV, No. 7 (March 1952).

Alphabetical listing by state, giving publisher, date last published, and price.

State Manual Procurement Guide (Hotaling, D. O.). New York, *Special Libraries,* August 1953.

Lists available state manuals, together with frequency and price. Contains advice on how to obtain them.

Trade Directories of the World, 1954-1955. Queens Village, N.Y., Croner Publications.

Loose-leaf publication with supplements. A descriptive list of such directories grouped by country and indexed by trade and profession. A noteworthy attempt to provide information in an area where it is limited.

Annuals, handbooks, special compilations

Cole, Arthur H., *Measures of Business Change.* Chicago, Irwin, 1952.

A descriptive list of 449 index series showing subject, compiler, frequency, period covered and basis on which the index is developed. Indicates regional and product indexes.

Encyclopedia of the Social Sciences. New York, Macmillan, 1930-35. 15 vol.

Outstanding authoritative information on background for many business subjects. Supplemented by extensive bibliographies.

Encyclopedic Dictionary of Business. New York, Prentice-Hall, 1952.

Alphabetical list of words and terms covering accounting, advertising, industrial relations, and other phases of business activity. Illustrative material, pictures, tables, and computations are given to supplement definitions.

Horton, B. J., *Dictionary of Modern Economics.* Washington, Public Affairs Press, 1948.

A selection of terms which most frequently appear in writings on our present economy, or which help to understand the past as it influenced the present, or are used in business and economics. Includes biographies of economists and statements on laws, institutions, agencies, government and private, and court decisions which have affected our economy.

Market Data Book Number, Industrial Marketing. Chicago. Annual.

Contains basic data on industrial and trade markets and the business periodicals and directories serving these markets. Gives format details and total circulation. Information supplemented by descriptive advertisements.

Trade-Names Index; with Definitions and Sources from a Card File in the Technology Department of the Carnegie Library of Pittsburgh and a Bibliography of Sources of Trade-Names and Trade-Marks. New York, Special Libraries Association, 1941.

"Concerned with definitions of materials, processes, and equipment of technical significance." References cited in most cases. Includes classified bibliography of sources.

Periodicals and services

Business Information Sources, Bulletin of the Business Information Bureau. Cleveland, Ohio, Public Library. Irregular.

A list of books, with annotations and periodicals containing the same subject matter. Each issue is devoted to one main subject with subdivisions.

Business Literature, Bulletin of the Business Library. Newark, N.J., Public Library. Monthly, September-June.

A monthly bibliographical treatment of current business questions. Includes annotated lists by subject of many business directories and periodicals and discussion of their uses and development. Cumulated bound volumes since 1934.

Directories

American Library Association. New York, Bowker. Triennial.

Classified list of 11,920 public, educational, and special libraries in the United States and Canada arranged geographically, giving statistical data and directing personnel.

Directory of Newspapers and Periodicals. Philadelphia, Pa., Ayer. Annual.

An annual guide to publications printed in the United States and its possessions, listing them geographically and noting publication date, general characteristic, editor, etc. Classified lists of agricultural, general and trade, technical, and class publications grouped by subject are included.

Editorial Directory. New York, Galub, 1953.

Lists business, industrial, and professional publications under interest groups. Alphabetical index. Descriptive note includes editorial personnel, editorial content and features, payment policy, and types of readers.

Handbook of Commercial, Financial and Information Services, compiled by Walter G. Hausdorfer. New York, Special Libraries Association, 1944.

A compilation of information on the coverage frequency of specific services supplied by the 577 organizations listed. A useful tool for the businessman, the student, and to both public and special libraries. Contains list of "Services No Longer Supplied" and index to the subjects covered by the 577 publishers.

Special Library Resources. New York, Special Libraries Association, 1941.

A descriptive directory of research library collections in the special library field and in public and university libraries. The arrangement is alphabetical under state, city, company, or organization name. The data includes location and date of founding, type of library, subjects covered, resources, and special services performed.

Ulrich's Periodicals Directory. New York, Bowker, 1947.

A classified guide to a selected list of current foreign and domestic periodicals. As the approximate number of entries is 7500, it serves as the key to many sources not generally noted. About sixty-five business subject classifications are included.

General texts

"City Directories as Economic and Sociological Records," *Business Literature.* Newark, N.J., Public Library, Vol. XXIII, No. 7 (March 1951).

Discusses uses and users, format, financial support, and function as tools in sociological research.

Coman, Edwin T., Jr., *Sources of Business Information.* New York, Prentice-Hall, 1949.

In this valuable guide to the use of business information will be found advice on how to find business facts and what timesavers to use for this purpose, references to sources on twelve aspects of business, and a recommended basic bookshelf.

Flexner, Jennie M., *Making Books Work: a Guide to the Use of Libraries.* New York, Simon & Schuster, 1943.

This book was written to help readers in the use of books and libraries. It describes in nontechnical terms the organization as it interests users, by explaining the use of a library catalog and books. The section on reference books includes business and financial publications, one-volume encyclopedias, trade directories, and special directories.

Hook, Lucyle and Gaver, M. V., *The Research Paper; Gathering Library Material; Organizing and Preparing the Manuscript.* New York, Prentice-Hall, 1948.

An invaluable guide for the individual about to prepare his first research paper, this pamphlet includes an annotated list of reference tools in the various fields of knowledge and detailed step-by-step directions on how to organize and prepare the paper.

Manley, Marian C., ed., *Business and the Public Library.* New York, Special Libraries Association, 1940.

A comprehensive study of this development by authorities in business reference service. Includes selected annotated list of business directories, magazines, and special reference tools.

Manley, Marian C., *Library Service to Business.* Chicago, American Library Association, 1946.

Covers the contribution even a modest business service can make to the community; library adjustments in setting up such a service; types of business information, how and by whom used; where it is found; interpreting the service to the community. Twenty-page bibliography, "Building a Business Library Collection," serves as a purchasing guide for the small library and a survey of such resources for the businessman.

Manley, Marian C., *Public Library Service to Business.* Newark, N.J., Public Library, 1942.

Discusses the development and use of business library service. Gives reports from specific public libraries in cities of 70,000 and over on the extent and handling of their business collections.

Government Publications

Bibliographies

"Business Observers for Federal Activities," *Business Literature.* Newark, N.J., Public Library, Vol. XIX, No. 5 (January 1947).

Descriptive list of services and magazines reporting government developments.

Business Service Check List. Washington, U.S. Dept. Commerce. Weekly.

List of material made available by the U.S. Department of Commerce in the past week. Many items are free material. Includes information on marketing data, small business, economic trends, foreign trade news, etc.

Hirschberg, H. S. and Melinat, C. H., *Subject Guide to United States Government Publications.* Chicago, American Library Association, 1947.

Under subjects are listed books and pamphlets published during the last twenty years. Material is selected for its greatest usefulness to libraries, and for its treatment of popular subjects. The latest available editions of annuals, etc. is listed. A bibliography of U.S. Government publications is included.

Price Lists. Washington, U.S. Superintendent of Documents.

These lists describe books and pamphlets available, giving catalog number and title. Publications are listed under subject. Those of greatest value in business are: census publications, which include statistics on manufacture, retail and wholesale distribution; commerce and manufacturers; finance, banking, securities, loans; labor, including wages, insurance, and compensation; and tariff and taxation.

"Priorities in Government Tools for the Business Man," *Business Literature.* Newark, N.J., Public Library, Vol. XXIII, Nos. 2-4 (October-December 1950).

Three issues featuring the most basic government publications. Sources of information and guides to use are listed as well as statistical compilations, directories, periodicals, marketing aids, foreign trade tools, and various important series.

"Put Your Business House in Order," *Business Literature.* Newark, N.J., Public Library, Vol. XIX, No. 9 (May 1947).

Annotated list of government publications of aid to the small businessman.

Periodicals and services

Monthly Checklist of State Publications. Washington, Library of Congress.

A record of those state documents received by the Library of Congress. Arranged alphabetically by state.

U.S. Department of Commerce Publications. Washington, Government Printing Office, 1952. Supplement 1951-52.

Catalog and index of selected publications of the Department and its predecessor agencies from 1790 to October, 1950. Supplement for 1951-52. Detailed index provides an excellent reference tool.

U.S. Government Publications Monthly Catalog. Washington, Government Printing Office. Monthly.

A list of government publications both congressional and departmental. Alphabetical arrangement by bureau or office, under department. Annual index. From July 1945, each issue has a subject and title index. Each number contains instructions for ordering documents.

Directories

United States Government Organization Manual. Washington, Government Printing Office. Annual.

Revised three times a year. Describes every agency of the federal government, legislative, executive, and judicial, giving latest information on organization and activities. Charts show organization. Index gives list of names and of publications.

General texts

Boyd, A. M., *United States Government Publications.* New York, Wilson, 1941.

Describes publication program of branches, departments, and agencies of the governing body, giving the history of organization, duties, and publications of divisions. Explains government printing, distributions, catalogs, and indexes.

Hauser, P. M. and Leonard, W. R., ed., *Government Statistics for Business Use.* New York, Wiley, 1946.

Outlines many statistical facts assembled by the federal government, and emphasizes their availability to potential users. Clarifies methods by which such data may be used as averages in measuring an individual business. Bibliography and index.

Leidy, W. P., *Popular Guide to Government Publications.* New York, Columbia University Press, 1953.

A descriptive list of some 2500 widely useful titles published 1940 to 1950. Arranged by subject.

Schmeckebier, L. F., *Government Publications and Their Use.* Washington, Brookings, 1939.

Describes available guides, indicates the limitations and uses of government indexes, explains the systems of numbering and methods of titling, and calls attention to some outstanding compilations in several fields.

Statistical Services of the United States Government. Washington, U.S. Bureau of the Budget, 1952.

Provides a general description of the economic and social statistical programs of the government—where they are located, how the data are collected, and what data are available in these areas from federal agencies.

INDEXES

Periodicals

Industrial Arts Index. New York, Wilson.

A monthly index to the articles in over 200 periodicals in the field of business, finance, science, and technology. Cumulated at intervals. Available in many libraries.

New York Times Index. New York. Bimonthly and annual.

Subject index to this newspaper, both daily and Sunday issues. References indicate page, column, and date, with section numbers added for Sunday issues. Brief summary is invaluable in locating dates of events and happenings, serving as a guide to articles in other publications. Annual numbers contain "outstanding events of the year" in chronological order.

Public Affairs Information Service Bulletin. New York, Public Affairs Information Service. Weekly.

A weekly index to current books, pamphlets, periodical articles, government documents, and other material in the field of economics and public affairs. Emphasis is on factual and statistical information. Cumulated five times a year.

Reader's Guide to Periodical Literature. New York, Wilson, Semimonthly.

An index to the some hundred odd magazines most often used in general reference work. Cumulated at intervals. Available in most libraries. Covers limited number of business magazines.

Maps, Atlases, and Gazetteers

Bibliographies

"A Time-Saver List of Sources for Maps for Sales Executives," *Sales Management* (Sept. 1, 1950). New York.

Presents a quick-reference summary of map sources.

Maps

Hagstrom's Street and House Number Maps of Counties and Cities. New York, Hagstrom.

Handy maps in four colors. When unfolded measure 29¾ by 33½ in., folded about 8 by 4 in. Each includes an index of streets and shows parks, airports, city and county boundaries, cemeteries, golf clubs, etc. Also indicates U.S. highways, main roads, state highways, surface lines, and turnpikes, and house and street numbers.

Polyconic County Maps. Detroit, Hearne Brothers.

These maps, 44 by 65 in. in size, are mounted on cloth and lithographed in five colors, with washable markable cellophane finish. Shows streets, avenues, roads, and boulevards within the entire areas, as well as railroads, parks, cemeteries, golf clubs, etc. A house-numbering system is given, and an alphabetical list of all streets, with mechanical street finder.

Atlases

Encyclopedia Britannica World Atlas. Chicago, Encyclopedia Britannica, 1952.

The political and physical maps of continents, countries, and states are given, followed by their geographical summaries. A section is devoted to world spheres of influence, geographical comparisons, list of abbreviations, etc.

Hammond, C. S., *New World Loose Leaf Atlas.* New York, Hammond, 1954.

Physical, political, economic, and historical maps in color. A *color key* indicates industrial, nonproductive, and agricultural regions. A *symbol key* shows principal mine workings and agricultural products.

Rand McNally Commercial Atlas and Marketing Guide. Chicago, Rand McNally. Annual.

Published annually, giving maps of all countries, with population, areas, climate, and other physical features. Also gives statistics on retail trade, agricultural sections, communications, mining and manufacturing, transportation, etc. Includes time-zone maps, air distance table, highway mileage map, and railroad distance map, as well as government bureaus and agencies maps.

Gazetteers

The Columbia Lippincott Gazetteer of the World. New York, Columbia University Press, 1952.

Invaluable encyclopedia of places arranged in one alphabet.

U.S. Official Postal Guide. Washington, Government Printing Office. Annual.

Lists post offices in alphabetical arrangement and by classes under state and counties. Describes organization of the post office department, use of mails, postal regulations, rates, etc.

chapter XVIII

Business Data Applied to Special Problems

Choosing a life insurance company. Appraising the residential aspects of a community. Analysis of two residential communities.

CHOOSING A LIFE INSURANCE COMPANY

What is the relative standing of a life insurance company? What types of policies does it issue? What rates are charged for these at different ages? What cash values are offered on various policies at different periods? What is the company's dividend record over a period of years? Does it offer disability insurance? The prospective purchaser of life insurance or annuity policy may find the answers to these pertinent questions in four basic reference tools.

Best's Life Insurance Reports and *Spectator Insurance Yearbook: Life Insurance Volume* cover much the same ground though they differ in format. These volumes give a brief but detailed history of each company as well as a critical analysis of its operation and management, its financial and statistical record, its officers and directors, and territory in which licensed. Here too are found significant ratios such as lapse, net rate of interest earned, average policy written, etc. The *Spectator Insurance Yearbook* differs from *Best's* in that it lists the classes of insurance written by each company. *Best's*, on the other hand, gives a critical analysis of each company's investments, a feature not found in *Spectator*.

For detailed information on a company's policies, *Flitcraft Compend* should be consulted. This contains rate, cash value, and dividend tables for each type of policy as well as information on age and amount limits, settlement options, restrictions, reinstatement, loan values, double indemnity and disability provisions, nonprotective provisions, etc.

Moody's Manual of Investment: American and Foreign; Banks—Insurance Companies—Investment Trusts—Real Estate—Finance and Credit Companies is useful for obtaining an over-all picture of a company's financial operations, the names of officers and directors, a brief history, territory where licensed, and sometimes the number of employees. Often too it notes the number of stockholders for a stock company.

These four sources may meet the needs of the average prospective purchaser. However, should he be interested in company facsimile contracts and actuarial tables for different companies, he will find the *Spectator Handy Guide* useful. Additional comparative data on current policy provisions and practices and types of insurance and policies is found in *Best's Life Underwriters Guide.* Illustrations of the cost of insurance are given in *Best's Life Chart,* which in 1953 covered 223 recommended companies. This lists also the principal items of each company's financial statement, although it does not take the place of *Best's Life Reports.* Where the *Spectator Yearbook* is not available, the same statistical, though not critical, material may be found in the *Spectator Compendium of Official Life Insurance Reports.*

Many fraternal societies issue life insurance. Some information on the companies is given in *Best* and *Spectator,* but more detail is provided in *Statistics—Fraternal Societies* and the *Consolidated Chart of Insurance Organizations.* The former has some features of *Best's* and *Spectator* and some of *Flitcraft.* Officers, date of organization, rates on policies at different ages, special features, and insurance statistics are given for each company. The latter covers 174 fraternal societies as well as 198 life companies and 12 life associations, giving financial and insurance exhibits, rates per $1000 for certain types of policies, names of officers, etc.

Other publications in the field are the *Insurance Almanac* and the *Cyclopedia of Insurance in the United States.* The *Almanac* covers both life and fraternal societies, gives organization data, officers and directors, types of insurance written, territory covered, financial and statistical data, and names of agents and brokers in the principal cities. The *Cyclopedia* gives brief information on life companies. Too, directories of agents and brokers for some states are published by the Insurance Field Company in Louisville in state editions.

Anyone wishing to keep in touch with company developments over a period of time would be advised to follow *Best's Weekly News Digest* and *Best's Insurance News* (Life Edition). Each has a section devoted to companies. *Eastern Underwriter, National Underwriter (Life Edition),* and others cover companies too, though not in separate sections. Many histories of life insurance companies are available. A more or less complete and descriptive list may be found in *Guide to Business History* by Henrietta Larson.

APPRAISING THE RESIDENTIAL ASPECTS OF A COMMUNITY

Companies frequently face the necessity of transferring employees from one end of the country to another. An important factor in the employee's decision to accept the transfer or to remain in a known environment is the possibility of congenial home surroundings in the new territory. In making the decision, an opportunity to compare information about specific conditions is essential, and besides the brief paragraphs found in encyclopedias, other sources of such information are many and varied.

The case of Mr. X who must consider a move to Fresno from Elizabeth illustrates the use of such data. Mr. X is married and has three teen-age children, so the quality of school facilities is a major question. *Patterson's American Educational Directory* lists the public school officials to whom he can write. There too he finds the names of the private schools and colleges. Since Mr. and Mrs. X are Episcopalians they look for a church of that denomination and find the answer in the *Living Church Annual*. The library is important to him, and the *American Library Directory* gives information on the number of volumes and the library's appropriation. Besides succinct information on Fresno, *Ayer's Newspaper Directory* provides the names of the newspapers published there, together with their circulation, frequency, political standpoint, etc.

Since Mr. and Mrs. X may want to buy a house, they will be interested in the tax rate, and may find this information in *Moody's Manual of Governments and Municipals*. Fire and police protection data is indicated in the *Municipal Year Book.* As for transportation facilities, the *Official Guide of the Railways* and the *Official Airline Guide* will show how the city is connected with other points, while *Mass Transportation's Directory* indicates local transportation facilities.

If Mr. X is fortunate enough to be able to consult a large city directory collection, the Fresno city and telephone directory classified pages will help him to determine what clubs, associations, theaters, recreational facilities, retail outlets, real estate agents, etc., are there. The street section of the city directory will give some indication as to which sections of the city are residential and which are business or industrial.

ANALYSIS OF TWO RESIDENTIAL COMMUNITIES

When a shift from one section of the country to another becomes essential, a comparison of data for the home community with similar information for those from which a choice must be made is desirable. An illustration of the factual information that may be assembled in order to provide a comparative picture may be cited from material on Montclair, N. J., and Webster Groves, Mo. For example, information found in Ayer's *Directory of Newspapers and Periodicals* shows Montclair as a residential city with some manufacturing of chemicals, paint, printers, and garden supplies. It has one weekly paper established in 1877 and designated as independent. Webster Groves in the St. Louis area is described as a residential town. It has one weekly Republican paper established in 1910. The *Lippincott Gazetteer* in its note on Montclair records it as settled in 1669 and incorporated in 1868. According to the latest census, the population was 43,927 in 1950. Moody's government volume shows that its tax rate is $64.80. Information on Webster Groves records it as organized in 1896; the population in 1950 was 23,390; its tax rate $34.30.

In relation to a standard of living comparison, *Sales Management* in its annual *Survey of Buying Power* is an important tool. This shows Montclair with an effective buying income per family of $8152 and a "Quality of Market" index of $141. On the other hand, Webster Groves with an effective buying income per family of $8984 has a "Quality of Market" index of $129.

One index to the impact of population shifts in the two communities is given in the *Real Estate Analyst's* report on residential construction for the years 1944 through 1952 which noted these comparisons:

	1944	*1946*	*1948*	*1950*	*1952*
Webster Groves	0	260	278	552	303
Montclair	74	179	59	203	39

An indication of the approach to health responsibilities is the listing in the *American Medical Directory* on hospitals. According to this, Webster Groves has a private nervous and mental sanatorium with 120 beds. Montclair on the other hand, is shown to have three general hospitals with 443 beds. As to the formal educational agencies, besides their public school systems, Montclair has a State Teachers College with a coed preparatory high school, a private boys' school and a private girls' school, two Catholic preparatory schools, while Webster Groves has a Protestant theological seminary, a Catholic Women's College, and two Catholic preparatory schools, one coed and one for girls.

Records of community support of another important educational agency, the library, show Montclair has 152,542 volumes with a circulation of 288,206. The annual income of $145,288 provides $87,255 for salaries and $27,087 for books and periodicals. Webster Groves, on the other hand, has a public library with 21,846 volumes but a circulation of 110,403. The income is $26,428, of which $11,196 is spent for salaries and $3035 for books and periodicals.

To turn to the representative people in the community, *Who's Who in America* lists sixteen residents of Montclair, while Webster Groves can claim seven names. In business leadership the last edition of *Poor's Register of Directors and Executives* with a geographical index lists forty-five Montclair residents and three for Webster Groves. Supplementing these statistical facts about communities, much information may be obtained from chamber of commerce publications and the volumes in the *American Guide Series* compiled by the Federal Writers Project of the Works Progress Administration.

part III

THE KEY TO SPECIFIC INFORMATION

How to Use the Index

The following is an author, title, and subject index to the publications mentioned or the subjects discussed in these pages. Those seeking information on the content of a volume or on the application of the information it contains are directed to the pages with its description in the annotated bibliography and to the discussion of its special uses in the general text or in the Appendix. All references to a specific business subject are listed. Checklists of the various types of publications noted are found under the headings Directories, Periodicals, U.S. Government Publications, Books, Services, Bibliographies, Statistical Sources, Reference Books, General.

index